T0328696

Cambridge Elements ☰

Elements in Research Methods for Developmental Science
edited by
Brett Laursen
Florida Atlantic University

PARCELING IN STRUCTURAL EQUATION MODELING

A Comprehensive Introduction for Developmental Scientists

Todd D. Little
Texas Tech University and North-West University

Charlie Rioux
University of Oklahoma

Omolola A. Odejimi
Children's Hospital Los Angeles

Zachary L. Stickley
Texas Tech University

CAMBRIDGE
UNIVERSITY PRESS

CAMBRIDGE
UNIVERSITY PRESS

University Printing House, Cambridge CB2 8BS, United Kingdom

One Liberty Plaza, 20th Floor, New York, NY 10006, USA

477 Williamstown Road, Port Melbourne, VIC 3207, Australia

314–321, 3rd Floor, Plot 3, Splendor Forum, Jasola District Centre,
New Delhi – 110025, India

103 Penang Road, #05–06/07, Visioncrest Commercial, Singapore 238467

Cambridge University Press is part of the University of Cambridge.

It furthers the University's mission by disseminating knowledge in the pursuit of
education, learning, and research at the highest international levels of excellence.

www.cambridge.org
Information on this title: www.cambridge.org/9781009211642
DOI: 10.1017/9781009211659

First published 2022

A catalogue record for this publication is available from the British Library.

ISBN 978-1-009-21164-2 Paperback
ISSN 2632-9964 (online)
ISSN 2632-9956 (print)

Cambridge University Press has no responsibility for the persistence or accuracy of
URLs for external or third-party internet websites referred to in this publication
and does not guarantee that any content on such websites is, or will remain,
accurate or appropriate.

Parceling in Structural Equation Modeling

A Comprehensive Introduction for Developmental Scientists

Elements in Research Methods for Developmental Science

DOI: 10.1017/9781009211659
First published online: July 2022

Todd D. Little
Texas Tech University and North-West University

Charlie Rioux
University of Oklahoma

Omolola A. Odejimi
Children's Hospital Los Angeles

Zachary L. Stickley
Texas Tech University

Author for correspondence: Todd D. Little, Todd.D.Little@ttu.edu

Abstract: Parceling is pre-modeling strategy to create fewer and more reliable indicators of constructs for use with latent variable models. Parceling is particularly useful for developmental scientists because longitudinal models can become quite complex and even intractable when measurement models of items are fit. In this Element, the authors provide a detailed account of the advantages of using parcels, their potential pitfalls, and the techniques for creating them for conducting latent variable structural equation modeling (SEM) in the context of the developmental sciences. They finish with a review of the recent use of parcels in developmental journals. Although they focus on developmental applications of parceling, parceling is also highly applicable to any discipline that uses latent variable SEM.

Keywords: parceling, latent variable modeling, longitudinal SEM, developmental research, measurement

ISBNs: 9781009211642 (PB), 9781009211659 (OC)
ISSNs: 2632-9964 (online), 2632-9956 (print)

Contents

1 Introduction

Latent variable structural equation modeling (SEM; Hoyle, 2012; MacCallum & Austin, 2000; Tarka, 2018) is a common data analytic method in developmental science. An important advantage of SEM is the ability to model multi-item scales as latent constructs. Advantages of latent constructs compared to other common methods such as sums or averages of items include correcting for measurement error, making minimal psychometric assumptions, establishing factorial invariance across time and groups, evaluating model fit, and broad flexibility for confirmatory modeling (Hoyle, 2012; Lei & Wu, 2007; Tomarken & Waller, 2005; Van De Schoot et al., 2015). The benefits of SEM and of using latent constructs can be augmented with parceling, which is a pre-analytic step done before estimating latent constructs. Parceling involves making aggregates of two or more items, and then using these aggregated items as the indicators of the latent constructs (Little et al., 2002; Matsunaga, 2008). In this guide, we first provide a detailed overview of parceling and its benefits. Second, we detail methods for building parcels, particularly in the context of longitudinal models and when dealing with missing data (a ubiquitous issue in longitudinal research). Finally, we review the use of parceling in the recent developmental literature.

2 Parceling: What Is It and Why Use It?

In the measurement model of SEM and confirmatory factor analysis (CFA), latent constructs are estimated by regressing each indicator on to its respective construct (Matsunaga, 2010; Violato & Hecker, 2007). Parceling is a pre-analytic step that is done prior to estimating the latent constructs. As already mentioned, when creating a parcel (sometimes referred to as a *testlet*; Thompson & Melancon, 1996), two or more items of a construct are aggregated (i.e., averaged or summed) before being used as the modeled indicators of the latent constructs (Little et al., 2002; Matsunaga, 2008). Accordingly, any multi-item scale can be reduced to a few parcels that would then be used as the indicators to estimate latent constructs. For example, a nine-item scale could be reduced to three parcels, each consisting of three averaged items, resulting in three indicators (parcels) rather than nine indicators (items) when estimating the latent factor (see Figure 1).

Parceling is increasingly used in developmental studies but remains underutilized in a majority of studies (see Section 5). The additional step of parceling has many advantages that warrant its consideration when elaborating analytic models that use latent constructs in the SEM framework, particularly in the context of longitudinal SEM. In the next section, we discuss the advantages of parceling with a focus on cross-sectional models, but every advantage generalizes to longitudinal research, and, in fact,

Table 1 General benefits of parceling (versus using items as indicators for a latent construct)

Psychometric Benefits	Model Estimation Benefits
Higher reliability	Lower indicator to sample size ratio
Greater indicator communality	Lower likelihood of correlated residuals
Higher common-to-unique factor variance ratio	Lower likelihood of dual factor loadings
Lower likelihood of distributional violations	Reduced sources of sampling error
More, tighter, and more equal intervals	Reduced sources of parsimony error

Note. Adapted from Little et al. (2002).

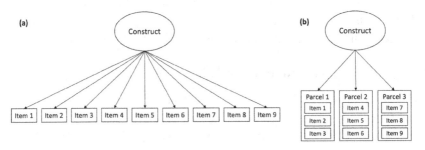

Figure 1 Latent construct with (a) nine item-level indicators and (b) three parcel-level indicators comprised of three items each. Variances, covariances, and mean structure are not included in the figure for reading ease

parcels have particular advantages for longitudinal models in their own right. For example, making complex longitudinal models more manageable, increasing the likelihood of achieving measurement invariance over time, improving model estimation efficiency (e.g., power, iteration speed, and likelihood of convergence), and others, which we discuss in more detail next.

2.1 Advantages of Parceling

Parceling can help address several problems that arise in item-level data at the psychometric level and at the modeling level (Little et al., 2002, 2013; Matsunaga, 2008). The main benefits of parceling are summarized in Table 1.

2.2 Psychometric Benefits of Parcels

2.2.1 Higher Reliability, Scale Communality, and Common-to-Unique Factor Variance Ratio

The advantages of aggregation have been discussed for decades, with the arguments for multi-item scales being closely related to the arguments for the use of parcels as indicators of latent constructs. The principle of aggregation states that aggregate scores are more likely to be representative of the construct of interest in contrast to item-level scores or single measurements (Rushton et al., 1983); moreover, aggregate scores are less biased and more statistically reliable because errors of measurement are reduced in the process. Aggregating items increases reliability, which, in turn, yields stronger associations among constructs that are theoretically related when they are modeled with aggregate scores rather than with single measurements or items (Diamantopoulos et al., 2012; Rushton et al., 1983). That is, "whenever there is the possibility of unreliability of measures, then aggregation becomes a desideratum" (Rushton et al., 1983, p. 34). The same logic, detailed later in this Element, applies to the use of parceling. Here, parceling can be considered partial aggregation of the set of items in to two or three indicators of the construct, whereas full aggregation would involve aggregating all the items into a single indicator. Full aggregation has the disadvantage, however, of not being able to separate true score information from measurement error and leads to attenuated estimates of any associations that are modeled. Multiple parcels, on the other hand, allow estimation of measurement error in the form of the residual variances of the parceled indicators.

From a traditional measurement theory perspective, item responses include several sources of variance: the desired true source of variance representing the construct of interest, as well as the undesirable variance that can come from a number of sources. This undesirable variance can arise from numerous effects such as method contamination, acquiescence response bias, social desirability, priming, and item-wording characteristics such as negatively valanced items, subordinate clauses, and common parts of speech (Little et al., 2002). By averaging items into parcels, the proportion of desirable variance related to the construct of interest is accentuated while the proportion of undesirable variance related to the effects listed above is decreased.

Both the principles of aggregation (Rushton et al., 1983) and foundational principles of psychometrics (McDonald, 1999) give a framework to understand the advantages of parceling. Figure 2 depicts a visual of the domain sampling model for selecting items to represent a construct. There are three fundamental assumptions of a domain sampling model under psychometric theory: (1) an infinite number of indicators exists in construct space; (2) a finite number of

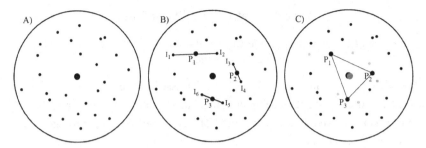

Figure 2 Domain sampling model of three parcels derived from six items. From Little (2013, in press), reproduced with permission of the author

indicators may be selected to reflect the meaning of this construct; and (3) each indicator will have some degree of relationship with the construct's true centroid and some degree that is unrelated to the construct as well as random measurement error (Little et al., 1999).

Panel A of Figure 2 shows six items that surround the construct centroid. The outer circle represents the potential selection plane of the items for representing the construct. Panel B shows the location of each parcel when two items are averaged. Specifically, the location is the midpoint of the line linking the two items being averaged to create the new parceled indicator. Panel C shows how the three parcels triangulate around the true construct centroid. In fact, the geometric midpoint of the area defined by the three parcels is the construct centroid that the parcels measure. In the case of the parcels in Figure 2, the parcels point to the true construct centroid (see Little et al., 1999 for examples of when indictors are inaccurate in representing the construct centroid). Figure 3 shows a different view on the possible selection planes. Here, the different selection planes vary in terms of their communality (i.e., the height of the plane indicated by the vertical axis of the figure). The horizontal axis shows the width of a particular selection plane. The width of a plane is orthogonal to the height of a plane. The width of a plane is the amount of reliable variance in the indicator that is unrelated to the construct (i.e., item-specific information). The distance of a selection plane from the outer arch represents the amount of unreliability of an item selected from a given plane. In general, when items are averaged, the new parcel moves closer to the construct centroid (i.e., has less selection diversity or lower specific variance, s – which we define more thoroughly later in this section) and moves up in terms of its communality (i.e., the true score, T, of the parcel – again, we define more thoroughly later in this section). For example, items with communalities of around .4 would yield parcels with communalities around .6 and much narrower selection diversity than the items had.

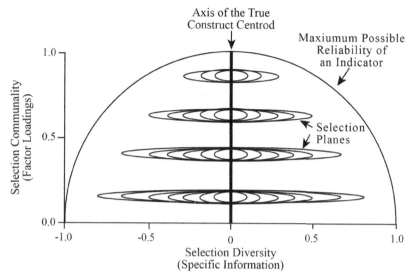

Figure 3 Side view of the domain sampling model showing various selection planes with differing levels of selection diversity (horizontal axis) and differing levels of communality (vertical axis). From Little (in press), reproduced with permission of the author

As already mentioned, modern test theory states that the score for any indicator, or variable, is composed of multiple sources of variance. Latent variable modeling seeks to decompose these sources of variance in order to increase the generalizability of a construct (Little, 2013). Modeling these sources of variance is important because some are necessary and desirable (i.e., the true score), and others are undesirable (i.e., the indictor-specific variance) as well as random noise in the indicator.

There are three general variants of test theorem tenets as shown in Equation 1:

Equation 1. Traditional test theorem variants

a) $x_i = T_i + s_i + e_i$

b) $x = T + s + e$

c) $x_1 = T + s_1 + e_1$

where x_i is the score for an individual i,

i is the index referring to an individual or unit,

x without subscript is the set of scores across all individuals and units,

x_1 is the set of scores for indicator 1 of a latent construct,

T is the "true-score" variance,

s is the item- or variable-specific variance, and

e is truly random error variance (random noise).

By definition, the true-score component, T, the item-specific component, s, and the error variance, e, are uncorrelated with each other within a score, X (Bollen, 1989; Little, 2013). A key assumption of test theory is that the s's and e's are uncorrelated with each other across all indicators both within a scale and between scales and that they have zero means. The true-score information, T, across a set of items for a given construct is, by definition, the shared information, or common variance, among the items of a construct. The sum of the item-specific variance and the error variance is known as the uniqueness of the indicator, or the indicator's unique factor. The uniqueness of an indicator is broadly referred to as the indicator's residual. The assumption about the independence of the s's is untested when scale averages are modeled. With latent variable modeling, however, it is possible for the item-specific variance of one indicator to have shared information with the item-specific variance from another indicator (e.g., shared wording between two items). When item-specific variances have shared information (after controlling for the common variance among the set of indicators), they can be allowed to correlate in the measurement model (i.e., correlated residuals are allowable).

Expanding upon classical test theorem, Equation 2 highlights additional sources of variance that can emerge, particularly in longitudinal studies. That is, the true score from Equation 1 can be conceptualized as having multiple components. In Equation 2, C represents the individual differences in the true score of the indicator that is constant across time (i.e., trait-like stability between individuals). Given that every measure is a combination of trait and method (Campbell & Fiske, 1959), M represents the potential of shared method-related variance in each indicator of a construct. O represents the change in the individual differences variance that can occur at a given occasion of measurement. Not represented in this equation is the within-person change (controlling for between-person differences) that can occur between two occasions of measurement. In longitudinal measurement, the occasion of measurement can represent age, time, or historical events. Longitudinal studies attempt to measure changes in the construct variance (O), without the influence of the stable construct variance (C), and when possible, without the influence of method variance (M).

When method variance is included in the measure of the construct, bias is present. When two constructs (or scales) are measured similarly, such as both use pencil and paper method or both rely on self-report, the construct variance now represents the shared true variance as well as method variance, and the correlation between the two constructs will be inflated. This method contamination also applies if one construct is measured with a teacher observation and another with student self-report. Here, the correlation between them will be deflated by the nonshared method variance. Although the source of variance or contamination is often difficult to determine when constructs have a similar amount and type of contamination, the relative differences in correlations among the constructs can still be meaningfully interpreted, even though there will be bias in the absolute levels of the correlations.

Equation 2. A broader conceptualization of measurement theory

$a)$ $I_1 = C + M + O + S_1 + e_1$

$b)$ $I_2 = C + M + O + S_2 + e_2$

$c)$ $I_3 = C + M + O + S_3 + e_3$

where I_n is the set of scores for an indicator n,

C is the stable construct variance,

M is potential common method variance,

O is the occasion of measurement variance,

S_n is the item- or variable-specific variance for indicator n,

e_n is truly random variance (random noise) for indicator n,

within an indicator, C, M, O, S, and e are uncorrelated (independent),

between indicators, only S and e are uncorrelated,

sources of variance are assumed to be normally distributed, and

only, C, M, O can have nonzero means. S and e have a mean of zero.

These equations show that item values are not a perfect representation of a construct because they consist not only of the "true" score reflecting the latent construct of interest, but also of the item's specific variance and random error (as mentioned, the sum of these latter two sources of variance are referred to as the item uniqueness or the item's unique factor). Because unique variance is a component of the total variance of a total scale average (or sum), regression coefficients based on the fully aggregated scale will be underestimated (i.e., attenuated; Nunnally, 1978). Additionally, the sum of the random error and the item-specific variance reduce communality among the scale items (Gorsuch, 1988).

The three sources of variance within items are captured in a factor analytic model of the item structure. Accordingly, the true score (T) is the variance shared among the indicators (i.e., T of each item) that defines the common factor (i.e., the modeled construct), that is, the information that we want to capture in the latent factor. Although T is shared between items, s_i and e_i are assumed to be uncorrelated with each other. As mentioned, the sum of s_i and e_i is referred to as the item's uniqueness. Theoretically, s and e should be uncorrelated with each other and have a mean of zero. Across all items in a pool of items, it is assumed that the s and e of each item are uncorrelated with all other items' s and e elements. This assumption is theoretically true for ε elements because these elements reflect the truly random error aspect of measurement, and must, by definition, be uncorrelated with all other ε and s elements. The s component of a given item, however, while uncorrelated with ε elements is unlikely to be truly uncorrelated with all other s elements. Accordingly, the common saying that " s is assumed to be uncorrelated with all other s elements" is not completely accurate. The actual assumption is that the s elements are only trivially correlated with other s's, and that they can thus be treated *as if* they were uncorrelated.

Aggregation through parceling preserves the shared variance (T) while reducing the variance related to item uniqueness, which is not shared between items. Thus, compared to items, a parcel score would have a higher proportion of true score related to the construct relative to uniqueness not related to the construct, making the score of the parcel more reliable than the score of individual items. As can be seen in Figure 4, a two-item parcel is expected to include the variance of the true score (T) plus one-fourth of each of the four sources of variance not associated with the common factor: (1) the specific variance of item 1, (2) the specific variance of item 2, (3) the random error of item 1, and (4) the random error of item 2. Thus, the variance of the parcel is expected to be equal to the shared variance of $T + \frac{1}{4}$ of the variance of s_1, s_2, ε_1, and ε_2. If three items are averaged, then each of the s and ε of the three items is reduced to one-ninth of their original magnitudes (see Little et al., 2013, for the proof of these concepts). On the one hand, since items aggregated into a parcel all measure the same construct, the T portion of variance is shared across items and captured in the parcel. On the other hand, since s and e are either uncorrelated or trivially correlated across items, both are reduced after aggregating in a parcel. Thus, by reducing the effect of item-level specific variance (s_1 and s_2) and random error (ε_1 and ε_2), parcels allow for a more accurate model of the true construct variance when compared to items.

2.2.2 Lower Likelihood of Distributional Violations

In addition to being more reliable than individual items, aggregated scores (such as parcels) tend to better approximate the distribution of the construct being

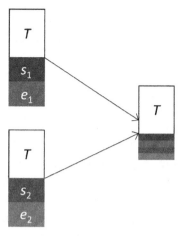

Figure 4 Variance of parcel composed of two averaged items. T = true score; s = specific variance; e = random error. Adapted from Rioux, Stickley et al. (2020)

measured than individual items (Boyle, 1991). In a multi-item measurement, each item usually measures only part of the construct (Rushton et al., 1983). Since individual items are expected to tap into a smaller portion of the construct than aggregated scores, their distribution is also expected to diverge more from the construct's distribution compared to aggregated scores, which better approximates the true distribution of the construct. Thus, even if a construct is theoretically normally distributed, items may show nonnormal distributions. When these items are aggregated into parcels, the resulting distribution would be more likely to approximate the normal distribution. The same principle would be true for constructs with nonnormal distributions, such as Poisson, exponential, or lognormal distributions (Galambos & Kotz, 1978; Joo et al., 2017). In line with this theoretical advantage of parcels, methodological research has shown that parcels can help remedy problems with nonnormal distributions (Bandalos, 2002; Bandalos & Finney, 2001; Hau & Marsh, 2004; Nasser & Wisenbaker, 2003; Thompson & Melancon, 1996), which can be an important advantage for analyses based on the assumption of normality. For a graphical depiction of this normalizing tendency of parcels, see Matsunaga (2008).

2.2.3 More, Tighter, and More-Equal Intervals

Parcels also have more, tighter, and more-equal intervals between scale points when compared to the scale of individual items. This advantage is particularly relevant in developmental science where many questionnaires still rely on the

Likert scale (Likert, 1932), which is essentially measuring continuous constructs with an ordinal scale. While one solution for this problem is at the measurement stage, where continuous measurements can be obtained using a visual analog scale (Rioux & Little, 2020), research suggests that although Likert-type items produce ordinal data, aggregates of Likert-type items are robust in analyses that assume the presence of interval data (Carifio & Perla, 2008). Thus, aggregating through parceling can help in having a more interval-level of measurement. Likert-scale items will only have responses at each integer along a Likert-type scale, a composite parcel based on an average will include values that fall between these integers, giving parcels a more continuous scale of measurement. By both improving the distribution of indicators (see previous section) and making ordinal measurements more continuous, parceling can thus, in many cases, allow the use of estimators based on the assumption of continuous and normally distributed variables (e.g., maximum likelihood (ML)). Direct ML estimation does not require some form of adjustment of the estimator such as using robust maximum likelihood or weighted least square mean and variance-adjusted estimators. That is, parcels reduce violations of assumptions for analyses with ML given they are more robust indicators compared to items (Lei & Shiverdecker, 2020; Li, 2016).

In terms of more-equal intervals of measurement, parcels harmonize the ordered categories to represent the response space with intervals that are more equal than the original items. For example, a four-point scale (e.g., never, seldom, often, always) represents the response space with rough intervals; that is, the distance between never and seldom is narrow in terms of the response difference, whereas the response space between seldom and often is a wider response gap. Parceling two items from such four-point scales would yield a seven-point scale with values that fall between the rough gaps of the original four-point scales.

2.3 Model Estimation Benefits of Parcels

2.3.1 Lower Indicator to Sample Size Ratio

Models with parcels have fewer indicators compared to using items. As such, the number of parameters estimated in the model is reduced. With larger models, this reduction in parameter estimates can improve model convergence and model stability (Little et al., 2013). This advantage is exemplified with a five-construct confirmatory factor analysis model, with each construct being measured with nine items (Little et al., 2013). A single time point and single group analysis of this model would have 3,825 degrees of freedom and 270 parameter estimates (not including potential correlated residuals and cross-loadings), which would be difficult to estimate even with a large sample. By aggregating items to have three parcels per construct, the analysis would have 80 degrees of freedom and 40 parameter estimates. This reduction in model complexity makes for a more manageable model. Because adding multiple time points or groups to the model would also increase its complexity, using parcels becomes even more beneficial to be able to estimate the model. Moreover, programming errors are minimized because the number of indictors to specify for each construct is dramatically simplified. This benefit is particularly relevant to developmental science where large models with multiple constructs and multiple time points are often tested.

2.3.2 Lower Likelihood of Correlated Residuals and Dual Factor Loadings

Parceling explicitly addresses problems of correlated residuals and unexpected dual factor loadings. Globally, this problem is addressed because parceling reduces the size of the s's (see Figure 4), thereby reducing the size of any correlation that an s may have with any other s in an analysis model.

The impact of parceling on correlated residuals depends on the parceling method. If two items with a correlated residual are assigned to separate three-item parcels, the size of the residual covariance between the parcels will be reduced to one-ninth of its size before parceling (Little et al., 2013). If the original residual covariance between items was small, that information may be reduced to a negligible size in the parcels and would most likely not result in parameter bias. If that residual covariance was large, it may not be reduced enough to be ignored in the parcel-level model. Alternatively, if two items with a correlated residual are aggregated into the same three-item parcel, the variance causing the correlation will not be decreased as much as when the items are assigned to different parcels. Indeed, in this case, the variances of the two items with a correlated residual would only be reduced to four-ninths of their item-level variance (Little et al., 2013). Because this covariance is isolated in the one parcel, however, this correlated variance component in the parcel does not covary with any other indicators in the model, and thus there would not be a correlated residual to include in the model with parcels.

Parceling has similar benefits for dual factor loadings (aka cross-loadings), which occur when an indicator of one construct also loads on another construct in the model, especially when the cross-loadings are on uncorrelated factors. Indeed, if an item cross-loads on an uncorrelated factor, it contains variance related to the uniqueness of the uncorrelated factor but no additional common variance, and when it is parceled with two other items, the unique variance that is related to the second factor will be reduced to one-ninth (Little et al., 2013).

When an item cross-loads on a correlated factor, there are more sources of variance involved. Here, the item that cross-loads contains both the variance related to the uniqueness of the correlated factor and the variance that is the source of the correlation between factors that all items are expected to contain. When parceling three items, the unique variance from the cross-loading item that is related to the second factor will again be reduced to one-ninth, but the variance at the source of the correlation between factors (that is shared between items) will increase to sixteen-ninths (Little et al., 2013). Thus, with uncorrelated factors, parceling reduces variance related to cross-loadings (one-ninth), which in many cases can allow the cross-loading to not be included in the model with parcels. For correlated factors, the variance increase because of the correlation between the factors is generally offset by the total reduction in the variances, particularly when the factor correlations are not very large.

To illustrate these concepts, Figure 5 shows an item-level solution for two constructs (Construct A and Construct B) that were both measured with six items (items A1 to A6 and B1 to B6). The item-level solution illustrated has one dual loading ($\lambda_{7,1}$), four correlated residuals within constructs ($\theta_{3,1}$, $\theta_{5,2}$, $\theta_{11,8}$, and $\theta_{12,10}$), and one correlated residual between constructs ($\theta_{8,6}$) that arise either due to sampling variability or true population effects. By aggregating items with a correlated residual within a common parcel, the effect of the residual correlations is removed by isolating it in the residual of the parcel. In our example (Figure 5), by aggregating items A1 and A3 into a parcel, the shared parameter (correlated residual $\theta_{3,1}$) would be isolated in the residual variance of the parceled indicator. Similarly, by aggregating items A2 and A5 into a parcel, the shared parameter (correlated residual $\theta_{5,2}$) would be isolated in the residual variance of the parceled indicator. The same would be true for aggregating items B2 and B5 (correlated residual $\theta_{11,8}$), and B4 and B6 (correlated residual $\theta_{12,10}$). Regarding cross-loadings and correlated residuals between constructs, as explained earlier (see section 2.2: *Psychometric Benefits* and Figure 4), parceling reduces the sources of variance that are causing these effects. In this example, there is one dual factor loading (item B1 is loading on Construct A; $\lambda_{7,1}$), and one correlated residual between items of different constructs (A6 and B1; correlated residual $\theta_{8,6}$). After parceling items with within-construct correlated residuals as described earlier, A6 would be parceled with A4, and B1 would be parceled with B3. Accordingly, the shared residual found between A6 and B1 in the item-level solution would reduce to one-fourth of its original magnitude in the parceled indicator. Through this reduction in size of the shared residual variance between A6 and B1, the correlated residual and dual factor loading would most likely be trivially small and could be ignored without introducing any bias in the results of the model with parcels. These

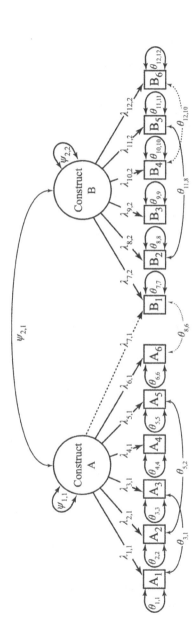

Figure 5 Item-level solution for two constructs each measured with six items

Note: λ = Estimated loading of an indicator on a construct. ψ = Variance of a construct. θ = Residual variance of an indicator or residual covariance between two constructs. ψ = Variance of a construct or covariance between two constructs. θ = Residual variance of an indicator or residual covariance between two indicators. Full lines are true effects in the population, dashed lines are effects found due to sampling error. Figure based on Rioux, Stickley et al. (2020).

benefits of parceling (i.e., the reduction of correlated residuals and dual factor loadings) feed into two other important benefits, which are the reduction in the potential sources of both sampling error and parsimony error.

2.3.3 Reduced Sources of Sampling Error and Parsimony Error

Sampling error is the difference between the true value of a parameter in the population and the value of the parameter estimated from a sample (Field, 2016). While sampling error differs between samples, it is usually larger in smaller samples, where it can negatively impact convergence and model fit (Anderson & Gerbing, 1984). When correlated residuals and dual factor loadings (discussed earlier) are found in a model because of sampling error, they should be ignored and left unestimated because they are not true in the population. Leaving correlated residuals and dual factor loadings unestimated, however, would treat these parameters, which are significantly larger than zero, as if they were zero. An unfortunate consequence of not estimating such a parameter is that it can negatively impact model fit and bias parameter estimates (Reddy, 1992). Including and estimating the correlated residuals and dual factor loadings would also be problematic since no theoretical reason other than chance could be offered to explain the observed relationship. Moreover, such a parameter could not be expected to replicate in a different sample. By reducing correlated residuals and dual factor loadings to be trivial enough to be unestimated (see previous section 2.2), parceling thereby minimizes the impact of sampling error on the model.

Although correlated residuals and dual factor loadings can be due to sampling error, they can also occur in the population. When correlated residuals and dual factor loadings are true population parameters, and if the phenomenon is unimportant to the theoretical model being tested, it would make sense to ignore these effects for the sake of parsimony in the analytical model. Ignoring these effects, however, can lead to parsimony error, where nonzero values that occur in the population are excluded from the model because they are theoretically uninteresting and presumed to be trivial. Because excluding these parameters increases discrepancy between the analytical model and the observed variance-covariance matrix, parsimony error can negatively affect model fit, while not usually affecting parameter estimates like misspecification would (Cheung & Rensvold, 2001). Just like for sampling error, by reducing correlated residuals and dual factor loadings to be trivial enough to be nonestimated without affecting model fit, parceling can minimize parsimony error. Furthermore, the parcel model is less likely to ignore true population-level correlated residuals and dual-factor loadings since the parcel model in the population is less likely to have these effects than the population item-level model (Little et al., 2013). Note that parsimony error and sampling error are not completely independent. Indeed, parsimony error can also itself be influenced by sampling error, where a small and potentially ignorable correlated residual or dual factor loading in the population is larger due to sampling error (Little et al., 2013).

Parsimony error also occurs when the nonestimated parameters (i.e., the ones fixed to be zero), which are trivially small in the population, are not exactly zero in the population. Ordinarily, these nonestimated parameters of a model (e.g., all cross-loadings of items for Construct A are not allowed to load on Construct B and the items for B are not allowed to load on A) are fixed at zero. In the population, however, all these nonestimated parameters will average zero, but few if any of them will be exactly zero in the population. In addition, all residual correlations are assumed to be sufficiently close to zero in the population such that they can be treated as if they were zero in the model. By way of example, one indicator, say A4, might have a population cross-loading of .09 and another indicator, say A6, might have population cross-loading of –.07. All indicators will have small cross-loadings, but this distribution of cross-loadings will typically have a tight normal distribution with a mean of zero. With parcels, the distribution of cross-loadings would become about one-fourth of the magnitudes of the dispersion of possible cross-loadings of the items when two items are combined and would be about one-ninth of the dispersion of the items when three items are combined. The example of A4 (.09) and A6 (–.07) presents a unique benefit of parceling. Here, if A4 and A6 are combined in the same parcel, the cross-loading of the parcel would be nearly 0, because A4's loading is in the positive direction and A6's loading is in the negative direction. These opposite valanced loadings would nearly cancel each other out and would completely cancel each other out if they were both of the same magnitude.

In the item-level solution for these items, these nonestimated cross-loadings produce some degree of model misfit. These nonestimated parameters are why (a) the model has degrees of freedom and (b) model fit information (including modification indices) is evaluated to determine if the set of nonestimated parameters can be treated as if they were zero in the population. In fact, if a model is true in the population, and it is fit to the population (no sampling error can occur), the model chi-square will equal the degrees of freedom of the model (cf. Widaman & Thompson, 2003). From this perspective, if a model had degrees of freedom equal to 129 such as the model in Figure 5, the chi-square should be 129 when fit to the population, and the model is true in the population. Model fit evaluation, however, does not rely on the chi-square test of model fit because the chi-square is sensitive to things like sample size and degrees of freedom.

As others have noted regarding SEM Models, "all models are wrong to some degree, even in the population" (MacCallum & Austin, 2000). Model fit evaluation, therefore, considers two sources of error when the recommended cutoffs (i.e., CFI >= .90, or RMSEA <= .08; see Little, 2013) are used to determine if a model is an adequate approximation of the observed data. One source of error is the parsimony error stemming from the nonestimated parameters and the other is the degree of sampling error that occurs for all parameters of the model, even the nonestimated ones. Here, for example, the true parsimony error of the loading A4 of .09 could also have sampling error around it. If the sampling error makes the loading appear as .15 in the sampled data, the loading would yield more misfit, but if the sampling error makes the loading appear as .04, for example, then the amount of misfit would be less for this particular parameter.

When parcels are created, each of these sources of error is minimized because the nonestimated cross-loadings and correlated residuals are all features of the specific variance of an indicator after conditioning on the true score that defines the construct to which the indicator belongs. Parcels reduce the influences of the specific variances of the items by canceling out through aggregation the information that was specific to each item that goes into a given parcel. Moreover, it does not matter which source of error is being canceled out in creating a parcel. On the one hand, a parcel is agnostic about the "true" nature of the specific variances. On the other, an item-level representation of a latent construct, such as in Figure 5, would need to consider each of the nontrivial correlated residuals and determine, through theory, which correlated residuals are true population associations and which are due to sampling error. At the item level, not specifying the true population associations would lead to model misspecification and parameter bias (e.g., correlated residual $\theta_{11,8}$). Specifying a correlated residual that is due to sampling error (e.g., correlated residual $\theta_{12,10}$), however, would also be a form of model misspecification, which in this case is called overfitting, and it too can lead to bias in the model parameter estimates. Because parcels are agnostic to the source of error in the item's specific variances, there is no need to make the determination of which are true in the population and which are not.

2.3.4 Benefits for Small Sample Sizes

While the benefits of parceling described earlier are applicable to research with any sample size, parcels can be particularly useful for research looking to fit structural equation models with latent factors in a small sample (Rioux, Stickley et al., 2020). Indeed, small sample size is a common reason for creating parcels (Williams & O'Boyle, 2008), mostly due to the increased reliability of the construct's indicators and decreased model complexity. As discussed earlier, parceling increases indicator reliability and factor loadings and reduces model complexity and the number of parameters estimated. In turn, these effects of parceling on the model can help decrease estimation issues and improve convergence (Bagozzi & Edwards, 1998; Barrett & Kline, 1981; Orçan & Yanyun, 2016; Velicer & Fava, 1998). Accordingly, a simulation study found that parceling may be particularly beneficial for small samples ($n = 100$ to 300), because results showed that parceling reduced estimation issues, decreased chances of misfit due to type I error, and did not introduce bias in parameter estimates and standard errors for structural coefficients among the latent constructs (Orçan & Yanyun, 2016).

2.4 Arguments against Parceling

As seen in the previous discussion, there are many benefits of parceling. A cursory look at the literature, however, will also show many arguments against parceling, which are thoroughly discussed in Little et al. (2002) and Matsunaga (2008). One argument against parceling is that it can hinder reproducibility and that results can vary depending on the parceling scheme. Parceling decisions should be clearly described for both transparency and possible reproducibility. Variability in results according to item allocation to parcels can also be examined and reported (Sterba, 2019; Sterba & MacCallum, 2010). Most other arguments against parceling center on differing analytic behavior and psychometric properties of parcels compared to items. A main argument against parceling is that when constructs are multidimensional/multifaceted, parcels can lead to biased factor loading estimates in the measurement model and muddy the interpretation of the structural relations in the model (Bandalos, 2002). This argument is true when parcels are randomly or improperly created, but when parcels are properly constructed (see section 3: How to Build Parcels), they can make the structure of multidimensional constructs more straightforward and facilitate interpretation rather than hinder it (Graham & Tatterson, 2000).

Another common argument against parceling is that it may mask misspecification of the model. This argument suggests that (1) because cross-loadings and residual correlations are more difficult to detect when using parcels in a model, estimates and other model parameters may be biased, and (2) since model fit is often improved when using parcels, analysts could falsely believe that there is no model misspecification (Bandalos, 2002; Marsh et al., 2013). Evidence contradicts this argument, however, with a simulation study showing that (1) parcel-level models produced similar or reduced-bias estimates more often than item-level models and (2) although parcel-level models had lower power than item-level models to detect within-factor misspecifications and single cross-loadings, they had higher power to detect multiple cross-loadings and structural model misspecifications (Rhemtulla, 2016). Another study also found that improvements in model fit are generally the result of a stronger measurement model (Landis et al., 2000).

Generally speaking, the thoughtful use of parcels and following recommended analytic steps are easy solutions to the potential misspecification problem. Data should be modeled at the item level to identify potential causes of misspecification and use the item-level information to inform the construction of parcels (Bandalos & Finney, 2001; Little et al., 2013; Rhemtulla, 2016). Moreover, local misfit in the parcel-level model can be examined, and the root mean square error of approximation (RMSEA) and standardized root mean square residual (SRMR) model fit indices can be examined as they were found to increase in parcel-level models compared to item-level models when there was model misspecification (Rhemtulla, 2016).

In general, the arguments against parceling often stem from a conservative-empiricist philosophical viewpoint (Little et al., 2002). This view of science argues that modeled data should resemble participants' original responses as closely as possible to avoid introducing erroneous data structures. In other words, any subjective decision must be avoided. And, indeed, avoiding the imposition of researcher bias onto data structures is a straightforward principle of science with which most would agree. Arising from this principle is also the conservative-empiricist thought that all sources of variance in every measurement must be fully represented in the multivariate modeling process involving a given scale. The assumption is there will be bias in the model's parameter estimates if any true source of variance is not modeled or included. Overall, these ideas emanating from this conservative-empiricist philosophical viewpoint automatically make parcels undesirable, since the creation of parcels from items inherently evades the objective nature of traditional multivariate modeling techniques and obscures the representation of all sources of variance in participant responses. This viewpoint has the implicit expectation of a well thought out theory of the items' specific variances in order to correctly specify which ones are true population effects (avoiding too much parsimony error when not estimated) and which ones should be ignored because they are due to sampling variability.

A liberal-pragmatic philosophical viewpoint would lead to different conclusions (Little et al., 2002). This view of science argues that experimental design and measurement operationalization are choices made by investigators within a rule-bound system. These choices are public and must be justified, reported, and considered sound by the scientific community (e.g., through the peer-review process and overall acceptance by the field). The liberal-pragmatic viewpoint also holds that representing *all* sources of variance from all items is impossible, and the goal of modeling is to represent the important sources of variance, which would be the common variance across items and samples. Thus, the conservative-empiricist viewpoint holds that multivariate statistical modeling should aim to represent all sources of variance, while the liberal-pragmatic viewpoint holds that multivariate statistical modeling should aim to build replicable models, which would be based on core constructs that replicate across samples. Thus, a data aggregation process such as parceling would be acceptable with clear choices and justifications. A conservative-empiricist views parcels as hiding the true meaning of data, and a liberal pragmatic views parcels as exemplifying model parsimony.

2.5 Conclusion

In the controversy surrounding parceling, the main factor determining whether parceling is appropriate or not is this Element's aims. On the one hand, if the objective is to investigate item behavior, parceling should not be done. A study that is developing a new instrument would focus the analysis on the behavior of the items, and the modeling decisions would involve considerable item-level theorizing. On the other hand, if the objective is to model the relationships among latent variables, parceling is a viable technique for recovering population values (Little et al., 2002). Parcels may be used because they provide psychometric strengths in models as well as improvements to model estimation (described earlier). Importantly, a parceling scheme should be justified and well executed, in addition to being transparently reported. The next section discusses methods for building parcels. Misguided parceling is never recommended, yet the benefits of appropriate parceling cannot be ignored. In the next section, we also generalize the above discussion of parcels to longitudinal models and describe additional benefits as well as caveats to consider when building parcels for use in longitudinal models.

3 How to Build Parcels

3.1 Number of Parcels

When deciding on the number of parcels to make, it is important to keep in mind the number of indicators needed for a latent construct to be considered identified. In order to estimate a latent construct variance, item loadings for each parceled indicator, and unique parcel variance, a minimum of three parceled indicators per latent construct is needed for each parameter of a construct to be just identified once a scaling constraint is chosen (Hoyle, 2012; Little, 2013). That is, a three-indicator parceling scheme gives each construct just enough degrees of freedom to estimate the unknown parameters that define each construct (i.e., making it a just-identified construct). Constructs with four or more parceled indicators will be overidentified with leftover degrees of freedom, which typically leads to an arbitrary improvement in model fit (Little, 2013). Overidentified models have also been known to be problematic when applying model constraints, because the orientation among item loadings (e.g., which items have the stronger loading relative to others) may occasionally shift. This behavior has been likened to a four-legged stool resting on an uneven floor that will rock back and forth, while a three-legged stool will not (Little, 2013). Accordingly, in our experience, a just-identified model with three parceled indicators is the optimum configuration for a parceled measurement model because it provides a stable foundation from which to specify the theoretically meaningful structural paths. This general recommendation does not mean, however, that a researcher cannot create a parceling scheme with a different number of parceled indicators if the particular measurement model requires it. For example, a construct that would be best represented by two indicators may be used (e.g., internalizing symptoms) or a construct measured by four distinct facets may then use four indicators (see discussion of multi-dimensional parceling later in this Element). Particularly in longitudinal and multiple-group models, two indicators for a construct is acceptable because the constraints to establish measurement invariance make the loadings and intercepts fully identified. In a single-group, single-occasion model, two-indicator constructs are underidentified although the loadings (and intercepts) can be estimated by borrowing information from other constructs in the model. The parameters can be fully identified by placing equality constraints on the loadings (and intercepts) and, based on simulation work, such constraints are, on average, unbiased (Little et al., 1999).

As mentioned, the ability to create just-identified construct representations for each construct has implications for model fit evaluation (Little, 2013). Recall that parceling items to create three indicators for each construct would remove any within construct degrees of freedom and yield a model where all model misfit is due to the between construct misfit. That is, with three indicators of a construct there are six pieces of information to inform the parameters of the latent construct (three variances and three covariances). With three indicators, there are only six parameters that need to be estimated after the construct's scaling constraint is placed (e.g., marker variable, fixed factor, or the effects coded method of identification/scaling). With two just-identified constructs, there would be nine covariances between the indicators of the two constructs that would be used to estimate the strength of the covariance between the two constructs. This model would then result in eight degrees of freedom. The amount of misfit associated with these eight degrees of freedom quantifies the between construct misfit in the ability of the estimated covariance to reproduce the nine between indicator covariances in the observed data. Parceling down to four indictors would yield overidentified constructs (an additional two degrees of freedom within each construct) and introduce seven more between construct covariances. Now model misfit would be a combination of the within construct misfit (which is typically trivial when parcels are used) and the between construct misfit (which would also increase only trivially when parcels are used). The model fit of a four indicator per construct model (using parcels) versus a three indicator per construct model (also using parcels) will give the appearance of very good model fit.

There are several methods to use when it comes to approaching the task of creating parcel-level indicators. The approach taken to creating parcels will very much depend on the dimensionality of the item-level data that are being parceled, and the theoretical framework motivating the parceling scheme. In the following sections, we will cover three unidimensional approaches to parceling data: random allocation of items to parcels, purposeful parceling, and the balancing approach to parcel creation. Then we will move on to methods of constructing parcels from items in a multidimensional framework. An overview of these methods can be found in Table 2.

3.2 Unidimensional Parceling Methods

3.2.1 Random Parceling

One method available for creating a parceling scheme for a set of items is random parceling. This method is typically best utilized when meeting the strong assumption that all items are interchangeable in the population, sampling variability is low (e.g., $n > \sim 200$), and is typically only recommended in cases of unidimensional indicators, or when one has a large set of items with high communality (i.e., high loadings in an item-level measurement model) from which to create parcels (Landis et al., 2000; Little et al., 2013; Matsunaga, 2008; Sass & Smith, 2006; Yang et al., 2010; Yuan et al., 1997). For this process to be done effectively, all combinations of items need to be generated and evaluated, and decision rules need to be made for what makes an optimal set of parcels (Sterba & Rights, 2017). This process can be computationally intensive and reflects a more exploratory process instead of purposefully engaging with data. One other proposed procedure of using the random assignment parceling method is to take the average model results of hundreds or thousands of item-to-parcel allocations, which has the added benefit of providing an estimate for the amount of parcel-allocation variability within the set of items (Little et al., 2013). Next, we present a simple simulation showing the variability that can

Table 2 Parceling methods

Unidimensional Parceling

Method	Description	When to Use
Random parceling	Randomly assigning items to parcel groups	When items are functionally interchangeable. Either when tau equivalence has been established or when there is a large sample of items with high communality
Purposeful parceling	Using information found in modification indices among items to construct parcels	After conducting an item-level CFA and evidence is found in the modification indices of correlated residuals or other problematic sources of variance that should be isolated into parcels
Balanced parceling	Pairing items with high loadings and items with low loadings to make parcels	When there are no problematic sources of covariance in the modification indices, or they have already been accounted for, the item loadings themselves can serve as guidelines to construct balanced parcels centered around the construct centroid

Multidimensional/Multifacet Parceling

Method	Description	When to Use
Facet-representative parceling	Parcel items based on shared secondary source of variance	This method is used for a multidimensional construct, when the goal is to model the implied higher-ordered structure that accounts for the common variance that the lower-order constructs share. This technique is also called homogenous multidimensional parceling
Domain-representative parceling	Distribute secondary source of variance across parcels	This method is used for a multidimensional construct when the goal is to model the pooled common multidimensional variance. This technique is also called heterogenous multidimensional parceling

arise when parcels are created randomly without meeting the assumptions previously mentioned.

3.2.2 Random Sampling Simulation Population Model

A population model (see Figure 6) was elaborated and used to generate simulated data based on a two latent construct design with six indicators each. The loadings in the population model ranged from .601 to .399 on the first latent variable, and from .602 to .398 on the second latent variable, with the latent variables themselves having a correlation of .60. In order to generate data that more closely resembles real data, we generated cross-loadings where the fifth and sixth items from the first latent factor load onto the second latent factor, with loadings of .40 and –.40, respectively, and added correlated residuals to select items that ranged from .20 to .50.

Using this model, a sample of 500 observations was generated using the simulateData() function in *lavaan 0.6–6* (Rosseel, 2012) in the R version 4.0.2 programming language (R Core Team, 2020) and the Rstudio environment version 1.3.959 (RStudio Team, 2020). Once these data were generated, they were converted into discrete value models with typical Likert-type 1–5 scale responses. Table 3 shows that these simulated data appear to be normally distributed and, without the usual worries of missing data, these data are well conditioned for our demonstration.

3.2.3 Random Parceling Demonstration

For random parceling to be considered an effective method, many random combinations of variables must be generated and evaluated for their performance, and some method for determining their effectiveness must be established (Sterba & Rights, 2017). For this demonstration, we constructed a list of all possible combinations of one through 6 items, since each of our latent factors was measured by 6 variables, which led to a total of 240 unique possible combinations of variables. Using this list, we systematically averaged pairs of variables together to create three parcels for each latent variable and evaluated a CFA model for each combination of indicators, capturing model χ^2 and its corresponding degrees of freedom and p-value, as well as the Comparative Fit Index (CFI), the Tucker-Lewis Index (TLI), the RMSEA, and the SRMR. Both latent variables had the same parceling structure (i.e., if MV12 was parceled with MV13 for the first latent variable, then MV22 was parceled with MV23 for the second latent variable, etc.), which would be the structure typically followed in longitudinal parceling strategies where the same variables are used at each time point for creating a parcel.

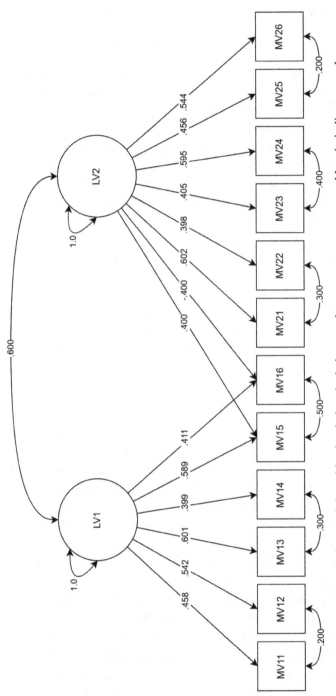

Figure 6 Population model used in simulation depicting two latent constructs measured by six indicators each

Table 3 Observed variable distributions

Responses	Items															
	MV11	MV12	MV13	MV14	MV15	MV16	MV21	MV22	MV23	MV24	MV25	MV26
1	19	12	2	16	9	15	16	3	10	3	6	7
2	206	193	84	162	116	201	189	148	93	74	114	149
3	243	252	293	276	248	244	236	266	247	273	258	287
4	31	24	116	43	112	39	58	68	140	138	118	56
5	1	1	5	3	15	1	1	5	10	12	4	1

The results from the random parceling are presented in the density plots of the selected parameters captured from the models (see Figure 7a–c). The χ^2 density plot has a vertical line indicating the eight degrees of freedom for each model. This plot, paired with the *p*-value plot, shows that even though most of the models were significant, there were a few models with nonsignificant χ^2 values, which is evidence that not all of the parcels are performing equivalently. This pattern is further evidenced by the CFI and TLI density plots, which each having a vertical line at the .90 cutoff for acceptability (Bentler, 1990; Little, 2013; Tucker & Lewis, 1973). The CFI plot shows that although a majority of the parcel-level models had CFIs in the adequate/good fitting range, some had excellent CFIs near 1.0, and others still had CFIs on the border of unacceptability. This range is even wider for TLI scores generated by the random parcels, where a majority of the models generated TLIs around the .90 cutoff, but some appear to be above 1.0, and some others appear to be nearing .80. This behavior only adds to the evidence provided by our χ^2 graphs that not all of the random parcels are behaving equivalently. Finally, the plots of the RMSEA and SRMR generated by these models show all SRMR values and a majority of the RMSEA values below the .08 acceptability cutoff depicted by the vertical line (Browne & Cudeck, 1993; Little, 2013), but some RMSEA values are closer to the .10 side of the continuum (which isn't uncommon for small models like this example), and we also see a small pocket of models with RMSEA values near 0.0, indicating that some models are fitting much better than a majority of the other models.

Where does this process leave us? We can select the parcels that returned the best model fit parameters, but would we be able to justify our decision making?

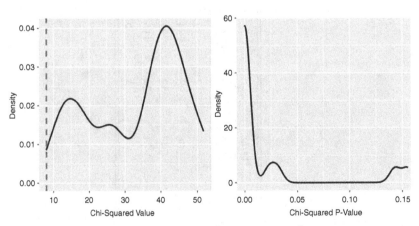

Figure 7a Random parceling density plots for χ^2 and *p*-value

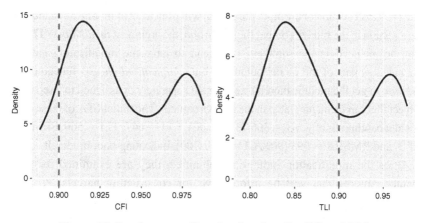

Figure 7b Random parceling density plots for CFI and TLI

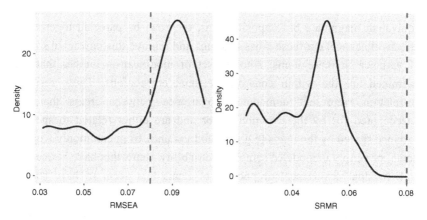

Figure 7c Random parceling density plots for RMSEA and SRMR

What if we get competing sets of parcels that have equivalent fit based on our testing? Using random parceling, we need to ensure that the rules set up to decide on a parceling scheme are defendable not just to reviewers, but also to the broader academic community. We must also be mindful of the limitations that such data-driven processes can have when it comes to generalizability.

3.2.4 Purposeful Parceling Technique

A more advisable approach for constructing unidimensional parcels is to use the information derived from an item-level CFA solution to inform parceling decisions. In most programs, it is possible to request modification indices as part of the model output. In *Mplus*, this requires including the command *MODINDICES* in the *OUTPUT* section of the input file, which will print a list of modification indices as a section in the model's output file. In *lavaan*, the argument *modindices=TRUE* can be included in the summary command to have the modification indices included as part of the model output, or the *modificationIndices()* function can be used to get the modification indices printed separately or assigned to a separate object that can be manipulated in the R environment. The initial CFA of these data yield a baseline fit of $\chi^2_{(53)} = 306.73$, $p < .001$, CFI = .647, TLI = .560, SRMR = .073, and RMSEA = .098 (90% CI = .087, .109), indicating poor model fit.

Once the modification indices are obtained, they are examined for particular patterns that will be informative for constructing parcels. Priority patterns are items that have particularly strong cross-loadings; if there are a pair of items that have a noticeably high cross-loading with another construct, they can be parceled together and allow this cross-loading to be estimated in the parcel-level solution, particularly if the cross-loading is theoretically expected. If there are two items with cross-loadings of roughly equivalent magnitude but opposite signs, they can be parceled together to effectively cancel out these cross-loadings and remove this unwanted source of variance in these items. Another set of modification indices that are examined are the within construct residual correlations. These residual correlations represent unmodeled covariance between items that are unaccounted for by the common factor and are either related to specific variance shared by the items (e.g., method variance from commonly worded items) or simply unmodeled sampling variability. Items that have noticeably high residual covariance, or pockets of items that seem to have shared residual covariance, are ideal candidates for being parceled together. When examining modification indices, the highest value is not necessarily the best candidate. Particularly with longitudinal models, consistent modification indices are more important than the absolute magnitude at a given time point and, as mentioned, reducing the impact of cross-loadings is usually a priority over the correlated residuals.

3.2.5 Purposeful Parceling Demonstration

We fit the CFA to the simulated data. Referring back to our previous demonstration, we can see the estimated model modification indices in Table 4 have two cross-loadings that both come from the same set of items but have opposing signs. Specifically, MV15 wants to load onto the second factor with an estimated loading of 0.361, and MV16 wants to load into the second factor with an estimated loading of −0.439. These two items' pattern of cross-loadings makes them prime candidates for parceling together, particularly if these cross-loadings are not supported

Table 4 Modification indices for initial model

Left-Hand Side	Type	Right-Hand Side	Mod Index	Expected Parameter
MV2	XL	MV16	66.246	−0.439
MV15	CR	MV16	66.245	0.287
MV13	CR	MV14	48.387	0.137
MV23	CR	MV24	47.777	0.183
MV21	CR	MV22	39.276	0.144
MV16	CR	MV24	26.446	−0.099
MV13	CR	MV15	21.375	−0.160
MV14	CR	MV15	18.741	−0.133
MV11	CR	MV12	16.698	0.080
MV16	CR	MV21	11.786	−0.069
MV25	CR	MV26	11.729	0.072
MV2	XL	MV15	11.690	0.361
MV23	CR	MV25	10.668	−0.084
MV22	CR	MV24	7.860	−0.064
MV23	CR	MV26	7.086	−0.061
MV11	CR	MV15	6.560	−0.074
MV21	CR	MV24	6.036	−0.057
MV14	CR	MV23	5.473	−0.051
MV1	XL	MV25	5.149	0.123
MV13	CR	MV21	4.429	0.041
MV12	CR	MV22	4.315	0.043
MV2	XL	MV11	4.074	0.106
MV1	XL	MV24	3.920	−0.109
MV12	CR	MV15	3.920	−0.062
MV11	CR	MV25	3.734	0.040
MV2	XL	MV13	2.946	0.091
MV11	CR	MV16	2.732	−0.032
MV15	CR	MV22	2.528	−0.036
MV16	CR	MV25	2.422	−0.031
MV15	CR	MV23	2.301	0.037
MV12	CR	MV23	2.284	−0.032

Note. XL indicates a cross-loadings, CR indicates a correlated residual. Mod Index is the expected change in χ^2 if that parameter was added to the model agnostic to any other change.

by theory. Here, combining them into a parcel would nearly cancel these values out, allowing them to be ignored in the parcel-level model and yet the parcel would still represent the construct of interest with no bias or misspecification.

To ensure a clear picture of the data are gained, we create this parcel, then reevaluate the model with this parcel replacing items MV15 and MV16 to see how the modification indices may have shifted. This new model has improved fit with $\chi^2_{(43)} = 169.88$, $p < .001$, CFI $= .755$, TLI $= .687$, SRMR $= .056$, and RMSEA $= .077$ (90% CI $= .065$, $.089$); the new modification indices are depicted in Table 5. By aggregating these two items into a single parcel, we've gained some ground in model fit, but we've also clarified the remaining strong patterns in our modification indices. Based on the patterns of correlated residuals shown in Table 5, we would aggregate MV23 with MV24, MV21 with MV22, MV13 with MV14, MV12 with MV11, and MV25 with MV16, which is represented in our final parceled model (Figure 8).

An evaluation of this final measurement model using the parceled indicators shows excellent model fit indices of $\chi^2_{(8)} = 11.92$, $p = .155$, CFI $= .977$, TLI $= .957$, SRMR $= .026$, and RMSEA $= .031$ (90% CI $= .000$, $.066$); the model parameters are depicted in Figure 8. With this measurement model, we have utilized parceling to isolate the problematic sources of variance to get at the constructs that are the primary focus of the research study. At this point, with a well-established parceling scheme, we can move into a larger SEM model knowing that the measurement model is no longer being obscured by these confounding sources of variance.

3.2.6 Balancing Technique

Another approach for constructing parcels for unidimensional constructs, particularly when there are no problematic residual variances or cross-loadings in the item-level solution, is to create balanced parcels based on an initial item-level CFA model. This technique involves using the output provided from the initial item-level CFA model to construct parcels that are balanced in terms of their item loadings by parceling the highest and lowest loading items together. With six-item constructs, the highest loading item would be used to anchor the first parcel and paired with the lowest loading item; the second highest loading item would be used to anchor the second parcel and paired with the second lowest loading item; finally, the third highest loading item would be used to anchor the third parcel and paired with the remaining, third lowest loading item. For example, for Construct MV1 in Figure 6, MV13 would be parceled with MV14, MV15 would be parceled with MV16, and MV12 would be parceled with MV11. If there are more items and the goal is to construct a just-identified three-parcel latent factor, the loadings are assigned in order of magnitude using the direction opposite the first to third lowest loading. That is, the items are assigned to parcels in a zig-zag fashion, with the fourth highest

Table 5 Modification indices for model with one parcel

Left-Hand Side	Type	Right-Hand Side	Mod Index	Expected Parameter
MV23	CR	MV24	55.105	0.204
MV21	CR	MV22	38.005	0.143
MV13	CR	MV14	24.737	0.148
MV11	CR	MV12	15.208	0.079
MV25	CR	MV26	12.622	0.076
MV22	CR	MV24	11.031	−0.078
MV21	CR	MV24	8.431	−0.070
MV23	CR	MV25	7.813	−0.073
MV14	CR	MV23	6.966	−0.057
MV12	CR	MV14	6.155	−0.053
MV23	CR	MV26	5.536	−0.055
MV11	CR	MV13	5.369	−0.052
MV1	XL	MV23	5.198	−0.139
MV1	XL	MV25	4.771	0.124
P13	CR	MV23	4.609	0.042
MV2	XL	MV11	3.937	0.100
MV11	CR	MV25	3.622	0.039
MV12	CR	MV22	3.384	0.039
MV12	CR	P13	3.348	0.034
P13	CR	MV24	2.872	−0.030
MV2	XL	MV14	2.869	−0.094
MV12	CR	MV13	2.868	−0.040
MV11	CR	MV14	2.742	−0.035
MV13	CR	MV21	2.585	0.031
MV1	XL	MV24	2.235	−0.085
P13	CR	MV25	2.032	0.026

Note. XL indicates a cross-loadings, CR indicates a correlated residual, P13 denotes the parcel created by averaging MV15 and MV16. Mod Index is the expected change in χ^2 if that parameter was added to the model agnostic to any other change.

going back on the third parcel, fifth highest on the second parcel, sixth highest on the first parcel, and so on.

This method can be used in conjunction with the purposive approach. Namely, after items with problematic loadings or correlated residuals are identified for parceling, the remaining items are assigned to parcels based on the balancing approach. Of important note here is that the number of items in

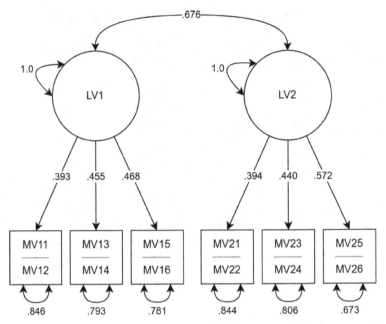

Figure 8 Parceled model of two latent variables measured by three parceled indicators each

each parcel does not need to be the same number and not all items need to be assigned to a parcel. For example, an eight-item scale of loneliness probably contains the quintessential item for measuring loneliness, "I feel lonely." This item, given its centrality to the construct centroid, could be left alone (not parceled) as an indicator of the construct. The remaining items would then be evaluated for cross-loadings and residuals and combined as needed. Here, one parcel might have four or five of the remaining items, while the third parcel might have only two or three, or the remaining seven items could be averaged to make two indicators. In other words, the number of items assigned to a parcel does not need to equal. Here, it's important to average the items instead of summing so that each indicator is on the same scale as the response scale.

3.3 Multidimensional Parceling Methods

Sometimes constructs are multidimensional/multifaceted in nature. Multidimensionality occurs when subsets of items share common sources of specific variance or the construct is measured by several groups of items that act as subscales, or facets. For example, the big five personality model assesses multiple facets of each of the big five traits (Costa & McCrae, 2008). Similarly, the child behavior check list assesses three dimensions of externalizing and two of internalizing (Achenbach, 1991). In cases like these, there are two parceling schemes that can be used to model multidimensional/multifaceted data in ways that can represent the multidimensional aspects of the items or isolate the sources of variance to get at the true score variance of the construct. The two approaches go by different names and have long histories. The first approach we call facet-representative parceling and is sometimes referred to as homogeneous parcels (Coffman & MacCallum, 2005), internally consistent unidimensional parcels (Kishton & Widaman, 1994), the isolated uniqueness strategy (Hall et al., 1999), and factored homogeneous item dimensions (Comrey, 1961). The second approach we call domain-representative parcels (following Kishton & Widaman, 1994) and is sometimes referred to as heterogeneous parcels and the distributed uniqueness strategy (Hall et al., 1999).

3.3.1 Facet-Representative Parceling

Facet-representative parceling is a method of parceling multidimensional data wherein items sharing a common source of secondary variance are parceled together in order to isolate the secondary source of shared variance within the parcel (see Figure 9a); that is, the uniqueness of each facet is isolated in one parcel. This isolation of the unique variance allows the shared common variance among each parcel to define the latent construct. In other words, the common latent factor captures what is shared among facets, while the uniqueness of the facets remains in the residuals of each parcel.

For example, a construct of intelligence could be created by administering a set of scales that measure intelligence such as the visual, textual, and speed subscales of intelligence found in a classic dataset of mental ability test scores of seventh and eighth graders (Holzinger & Swineford, 1939). In order to create facet-representative parcels, a parcel of the visual items, a parcel of the textual items, and a parcel of the speed items would be created and used as the three parcel indicators to estimate a latent construct of general intelligence (see Figure 9a). Facet-representative parceling is an implicit way to estimate a model that would sometimes be estimated as a higher-order construct (e.g., Bodin et al., 2009; Castellanos-Ryan & Conrod, 2011; DeYoung, 2006; Iliceto & Fino, 2017; Keith et al., 2006; Massé et al., 1998; Montigny et al., 2013). In a higher-order model, items/ scores of the subfacets load on their respective lower-order constructs, which in turn load on a higher-order common factor. This approach to modeling the dimensionality of the construct would be based on the

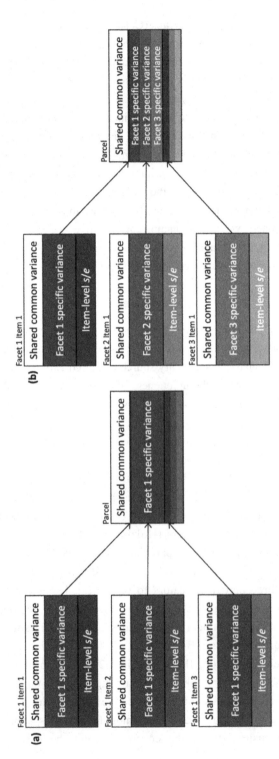

Figure 9 Variance of (a) a facet-representative parcel composed of three averaged scores from the same facet of a multidimensional scale and (b) a domain-representative parcel composed of three averaged scores, one from each of three facets of a multidimensional scale. s = specific variance; e = random error

underlying theory that the common, higher-order factor predicts the lower-order factors (facets), which in turn predict responses on the items (Byrne, 2005). Note that the lower-order constructs could also be represented with parceled indicators if there are more than three scores to represent the lower-order constructs.

Returning to our previous example using an intelligence scale with facets, a higher-order factor model would have visual scores loading onto a visual construct, textual scores onto a textual construct, and speed scores onto a speed construct, and the visual, textural, and speed constructs would load onto a higher-order general intelligence construct to represent the common variance shared by the lower-order constructs (see Figure 10b). In a similar vein, the twenty-nine items of the dimensions of internalizing from the CBCL could be parceled into three indicators of the Anxious facet, three indicators of the Withdrawn facet, and three indicators of the Somatic facet. These lower-order constructs would then load on a higher-order construct of Internalizing.

The choice between a higher-order factor model and a facet-representative parcel model is based on the research questions and the overall SEM model in which the constructs are being included. With facet-representative parceling, this higher-order structure is implicitly represented in a single-order model, which is a more parsimonious model that requires fewer parameters to estimate. Thus, if the focus is on modeling relationships among just higher-order constructs, this implicit higher-order model achieved through facet-representative parceling is the advisable path to take for model parsimony. Here, the idea is to create unidimensional parcels that represent each dimension or facet of the higher-order construct of interest.

Higher-order factor models are particularly tricky to specify and estimate with longitudinal data because the lower-order constructs' residual variances are uncorrelated with the higher-order construct (see Figure 10). With multiple time points the high-order construct at one time point may have associations with residual variances of the lower-order constructs at another time point. In addition, the between time associations among the lower-order constructs would need to be properly specified in a longitudinal structural model and decisions about where the mean structures would be estimated would need to be made. Moreover, convergence and empirical underidentification issues arise with complex decompositions such as a multi-wave higher-order decomposition. A facet-representative parceling scheme dramatically simplifies the modeling by focusing attention on the variance of the higher-order construct and placing the mean structures as the mean of the higher-order construct. Note that the means and variances of the Intelligence example shown in Figure 10 would

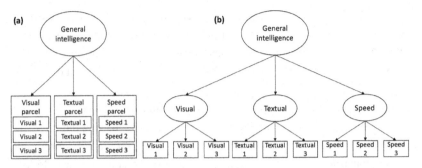

Figure 10 Representation of (a) a facet-representative parceling strategy to modeling general intelligence and (b) a higher-order latent factor strategy to modeling Intelligence. Variances, covariances, and mean structure are not included in the figure for reading ease

be identical across the two estimations when the mean structure is estimated at the higher-order level.

If, however, the lower-order constructs are of theoretical interest and are being included in a larger SEM model, then the higher-order factor model would be a better choice, particularly in cross-sectional models. If there are more than three items/scores per facet, then parceling could also be used within the lower-order constructs. Finally, if only some of the lower-order constructs are of interest in the larger model, it would also be possible to maintain the explicit item-level factor structure for the lower-order constructs being used in the SEM model while parceling the facets that are not, giving the higher-order factor a combination of parceled indicators and lower-order latent factors as indicators.

3.3.2 Domain-Representative Parceling

Domain-representative parceling is a method to address multidimensional items that could be considered the opposite of facet-representative parceling. Instead of grouping items from the same facet together, they can be spread out evenly among the parcels, thereby evenly distributing the secondary sources of variance (Hall et al., 1999; Kishton & Widaman, 1994; and see Figure 10b). Domain-representative parceling is a method of creating parcels that contain items representing each domain of variance across the multidimensional item set, which results in a common factor that represents the domain of the multidimensional variance across all items within the item set. With this method of parceling multidimensional data, items that share a common source of secondary shared variance, usually representing other sources of common variance such as subscales within the construct measure, are used to create parcels that each has a component of that secondary source of variance, ensuring that this secondary source of variance is spread out among the parcels. In so doing, this secondary source of variance will become common among parcels and will be combined along with the original common variance the items had in estimating the latent common factor. This approach is recommended when each of the sources of specific facet variance is expected to be related to other constructs in the larger SEM model above and beyond the common variance each facet shares (Kishton & Widaman, 1994; Little et al., 2013).

Returning to our example of intelligence as measured by Holzinger and Swineford (1939), we would create parcels that each had one visual, one textual, and one speed score averaged together (see Figure 11). When estimating the model with the three domain-representative parcel indicators, we would get a common factor representing a combination of visual, textual, and speed facets along with the general intelligence variance (i.e., the common variance these facets shared). In a study comparing these two approaches using an Internal-External Locus of Control construct (Kishton & Widaman, 1994), the domain-representative method outperformed the unidimensional (i.e., facet-representative) approach. More specifically, creating parallel indictors (akin to parallel forms) captured the broader construct space of Locus of

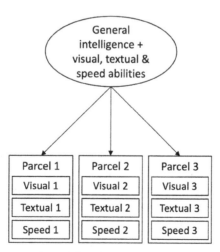

Figure 11 Representation of domain-representative parceling strategy to modeling a latent factor of general intelligence and its subfacets. Variances, covariances, and mean structure are not included in the figure for reading ease

Control better than did the common variance perspective inherent in the facet-representative parceling method.

3.3.3 A Priori Designs

A final method that can be used to allocate items to parcels is to use measures originally designed with parceling in mind. As we begin to think about how we collect data, one element to consider is either choosing a measure of our construct of interest that has an existing parceling structure or designing a measure for the construct with parceling in mind from the beginning. Designing measures with parceling in mind helps be more aware of the types of questions we're asking our participants, whether they are unidimensional or multidimensional in nature, and what potential sources of variance we can account for. Knowing that our target number of parceled indicators for a construct is three gives us a good starting point for the number of questions that could be included in a measure, with multiples of three being a good rule of thumb. If there are subscales within a measure, each of the subscales should have at least three indicators as well. An example of a measure that has been designed with parceling in mind is the Control, Agency, and Means-Ends Interview (CAMI; Little et al., 1995) that contains six items for each construct, three positively worded items and three negatively worded items. As part of the survey design, parceling instructions are included and suggest that researchers create parcels by pairing a positively worded item with a negatively worded item after it has been reverse-coded, thus reducing the negativity versus positivity bias as well as acquiescence bias present in the responses (Little et al., 1995; Weijters & Baumgartner, 2021).

A priori recommendations should not be blindly followed, and it is important to be mindful of the data by verifying that the expected covariance patterns are present before parceling. If there are some conditions in which the expected orientation of variables does not come out as expected, then the a priori parceling recommendations would not be valid for the particular data sample. Such deviations from expected covariance structures could be an indication of something as simple as mislabeling in the dataset, or something as significant as an item or construct behaving differently in the population sampled compared to the population sampled for the construction of the original guidelines.

4 Longitudinal Models

Although most of the examples presented so far have been simplified and are cross-sectional in nature, the fundamental principles of parceling can also be applied to longitudinal study designs, which is essential as these designs are foundational to developmental research, which relies on longitudinal data. With this in mind, a major consideration that needs to be made when parceling in a longitudinal framework is to use the same parceling scheme at all time points. This step entails building parcels that reflect not only the best parceling scheme at any one time point, but also the best parceling scheme across all time points. In order to do so, the factor loadings and modification indices in an item-level CFA must be examined to ensure that the criteria being used to construct the parcels are similar across all points of measurement and are not a feature of a single time point.

One method of approaching parcel construction in a longitudinal framework is to first establish metric invariance, sometimes called weak or loading invariance, across all time points. Invariance testing (Little, 2013; Van De Schoot et al., 2015; Widaman et al., 2010) is a process of applying systematic constraints on the model to ensure that the differences between the times of measurement are due to a real difference in the true score, and not an artifact of the measurement process. Invariance begins with an unconstrained configural model where parameter estimates are allowed to differ between groups or time points, and then the item loadings are constrained to be equivalent across time (and groups, if applicable) to establish metric invariance. If the model passes this test of invariance, scalar invariance (aka strong or intercept invariance) is tested by additionally constraining the item intercepts to be equivalent across groups or across time. When invariance holds, it means that the items have the same psychometric properties at all occasions.

The process of establishing longitudinal invariance begins with specifying the proper null model. The null model that is estimated by default in nearly all SEM packages and programs is not correct in a longitudinal framework, because it does not force the means and variances to be equal across time (i.e., the null hypothesis needs to include the assumption that there is no change across time in the means and variances). Because the default null in most SEM software can't be changed (as of this writing, the only exception is the lavaan SEM package in R), the proper longitudinal null model needs to be defined by hand (Widaman & Thompson, 2003). Once the proper null model has been estimated, all relevant fit measures can be recalculated with the correct null model chi-square and degrees of freedom. This correct fit information is used to evaluate the relative fit measures of each tested model.

Once the configural model is deemed a good fitting model, we test for metric invariance by constraining each of the corresponding item loadings to be equal across all time points. We recommend using the change in CFI of .01 or less to determine if these model constraints are tenable (Cheung & Rensvold, 2001; Little, 2013). If the weak invariance model passes, then there is a good foundation for determining a longitudinal parcel allocation, because the item loadings are psychometrically equivalent at each time point. We recommend examining the modification indices for potential sources of item cross-loadings or residual covariance that are consistent at each time point and use this information as well as the magnitude of the item loadings themselves to construct a single optimal parceling scheme that is applied at each time point.

Another way to find an optimal parcel solution is to stack the data by time and fit the item-level CFA to the stacked data. This approach is useful when invariance across time is confirmed but the pattern of loadings is not consistent enough to "see" a parceling scheme that would work across each time point. Stacking the data and then fitting the item-level CFA provides loadings that are harmonized across all time points and would give a pattern of loadings that has a strong likelihood of being the best for each time point.

A few general remarks about parceling are warranted in this section on longitudinal models. First, as intimated earlier, we recommend taking item averages instead of item sums in order to retain the metric of the response scale across all parcels. When the effects-coded scaling constraint is used, the mean of the latent construct would be equal to the mean of the items, and the variance of the construct would reflect the average contribution of each parcel in defining the latent construct (i.e., the average variance explained in each parcel). The mean of the construct would reflect the meaning metric of the response scale or a meaning transformation of the original response scale (e.g., proportion of maximum scoring; Little, 2013). With effects-coded scaling, modeling mean-level trajectories, for example, can be done on the latent construct means and would reflect the metric of the observed means (Little, 2013).

Second, and mentioned earlier but elaborated more here, the number of items assigned to a parcel does not have to be the same for each parcel (and sometimes equal items per parcel is impossible). In this regard, it is also okay to have some indicators be items that are not assigned to a parcel. This situation occurs, for example, when there are only four or five items to work with. With four items, a single parcel could be created from among the four items, particularly if two of the items have good loadings and two are on the weaker side; here, the two weaker ones would be good candidates to parcel together. Sometimes with only four items creating two parcels of that construct may be warranted. Even scales that have six or more items might warrant a parceling scheme where one of the indicators is an item and the other two are parcels created from the remaining items. This scenario can happen when there is a quintessential item for defining the construct. For example, the loneliness scale mentioned earlier would have "I feel lonely" as one of the items, whereas other items might read "I feel left out of the group," "I feel nobody likes me," and so on. Keeping the item, "I feel lonely" would make good sense because it is at the core of the construct and would likely have a strong item-level loading. As an aside, the two other example items would likely have a correlated residual in an item-level solution because they share the social isolation aspect of loneliness and therefore would be good candidates to parcel together.

Third, parcels can be created to address item-level noninvariance of certain items such that the parcel shows invariance over time (or across groups). For example, an item that has a loading that is lower than expected given the results of the invariance testing process can be paired with an item that has a larger loading than expected (or even as expected but one that is a strong item). Keeping in mind that a failure of invariance stems from the specific variance of the item and not the item's true score, reducing the specific variance that is responsible for the lower loading will minimize the lack of invariance. Pairing opposite valanced items would reduce the lack of invariance of the items even more such that the parcel would now be invariant.

4.1 Dealing with Missing Data

As anyone who has dealt with data gathered in the real world knows, missing data are inevitable. When data go missing, they go missing for a reason. The most widely used classification system for why data go missing details three general mechanisms by which data go missing using labeling that is unfortunately confusing to those not well versed in the world of missing data (Rubin, 1976; Seaman et al., 2013). The most misunderstood of these mechanisms explaining why data go missing is referred to as missing at random (MAR) and is used to classify instances where the probability of an observation going missing on a given variable is related to some other measured variable or set of variables in the dataset. Modern methods of treating missing data (e.g., multiple imputation or MI and full information maximum likelihood or FIML) assume that missing values have gone missing due to a MAR mechanism and use the available information from the variables associated with the missingness in the data to perform their estimations. When the variables associated with the missingness are included as part of the estimation process, the estimates are adjusted to be closer to what they should have been had there not been missing data in the first place.

Another mechanism by which data go missing is truly based on random chance and is referred to as missing completely at random (MCAR). In these cases, the probability that the observation has gone missing is unrelated to any other variable in the dataset, nor the value of the missing observation itself. There could be any number of reasons that data could be MCAR. For example, a participant may not be present at the time of the evaluation due to illness or having moved, or a participant may accidentally skip over a question when taking a survey. MCAR data would also occur when participants have been randomly assigned to have missing items or assessments within a planned missing data design (Little & Rhemtulla, 2013; Rhemtulla & Hancock, 2016; Rioux, Lewin et al., 2020).

The final mechanism by which data go missing is known as missing not at random (MNAR) and describes the case in which the probability of the observation being missing is related to the value of the observation itself, even after controlling for all other variables. An example of MNAR missingness would be asking for participant income. This question would be MNAR when high-income earners are less likely to provide answers, and there are no other variables in the dataset that predict this pattern of missing data. Thus, one way to proactively address problems with MNAR data is to identify items that may be sensitive to MNAR responses and provide additional questions that may be correlated with these items, which would convert the MNAR to a MAR process. Following our income example, we could ask related questions such as education level, profession, number of vacations taken in the previous year, number of cars owned, or postal code of residence which could be combined with census data before imputation.

Understanding the mechanisms of missing data is important because of the potential implications each mechanism has on how a researcher approaches their data analysis. If a person on the upper end of the income range did not provide income information, then our distribution of observed values is missing observations on the upper tail, and any regressions using income as a predictor will be biased due to missingness. If we can recover the missing values due to the presence of MAR mechanisms within our data, then we can reduce the bias caused by the missing data. On the one hand, some methods for dealing with missing data, the most prevalent being deletion techniques, single imputation, and last observation carried forward (Lang & Little, 2018; Rioux & Little, 2021), bias the results of any analyses and should be avoided. On the other hand, modern missing data treatments such as MI and FIML estimation have been shown to adequately recover missing information under both MAR and MCAR conditions (Enders, 2010; Lang & Little, 2018; Rioux & Little, 2021) and should be favored to recover power and minimize bias in the results.

4.1.1 Multiple Imputation

Multiple imputation is a missing data treatment done before conducting the planned data analyses (Enders, 2010, 2017; Murray, 2018; Van Buuren, 2018). It uses the existing variance and covariance relationships in a dataset to predict probable values for missing observations in the data in a systematic way that returns several imputed datasets (that represent a distribution of possible values for the missing observations). Data analyses are then run on the multiple datasets and parameter estimates are aggregated using Rubin's rules (Rubin, 1987). In addition to all variables to be included in the analytic model, variables associated with the MAR mechanism must be included in the imputation model to recover missing values and minimize bias (Collins et al., 2001; Howard et al., 2015; Madley-Dowd et al., 2019; Yoo, 2009). Although little research has examined how different imputation steps influence results with parcels, research on item-level missing data when computing scales can be informative as it also relates to imputation when aggregation of items is planned.

Imputation can be done before or after parceling, depending on the needs. When computing scales, a study showed that imputing before or after computing scales did not influence bias, but imputing at the scale level required a 75 percent increase in sample size to achieve the same power as imputing at the item level (Gottschall et al., 2012). If these results generalize to parcels, it means that imputing at the item level *before* parceling would increase power. One reason that imputing at the item-level leads to more power is that within-scale correlations are stronger than between-scale correlations. It is possible, however, that the power advantage of item-level imputation would be lower for parcels than for scales because between-parcel correlations mirror the within-scale correlations among the items (Rioux, Stickley et al., 2020) and may even provide more power than item-level imputation because of all the psychometric advantages for using parcels as indicators instead of items. Still, it would remain advisable to favor item-level imputation, because it has the advantage of providing more variance information to inform possible MAR mechanisms within the data. Imputing at the parcel level would become advantageous and advisable for datasets with a large number of variables. Indeed, the number of cases (e.g., participants) in an imputation model must exceed the number of variables being imputed and if a dataset has more variables than it does observations, then parceling can also be a method to reduce the size of the dataset before imputation (Eekhout et al., 2018).

4.1.2 Full Information Maximum Likelihood

FIML estimation is a one-step model-based technique where missing data are handled within the data analyses (Enders, 2001, 2010). FIML uses the existing variance and covariance information in the observed variables included in the model to provide parameter estimates in the presence of the missing data. Maximum likelihood is used to estimate parameters and standard errors while taking into consideration all observed variables for each case. It is important to note that FIML only uses variables provided in the model itself and variables provided in a list of auxiliary variables for estimating model parameters. Accordingly, to minimize bias, any variable that may be predictive of MAR-related missingness needs to be included in the auxiliary variables if they are not part of the analytic model (Collins et al., 2001; Enders, 2008; Graham, 2003; Howard et al., 2015).

With regard to using FIML when parceling in the presence of missing data, again methodological research on the issue is lacking, but research on item-level missing data when computing scales can be used as a guide. A study found that using scales computed from item-level data with missingness without adding auxiliary variables for missing data handling led to highly biased parameters. This bias was avoided if the individual items were included as auxiliary variables. Furthermore, this method of using FIML with scales in the analytical model and individual items as auxiliary variables was equivalent to item-level imputation in terms of power (Mazza et al., 2015). Still, this method could have drawbacks because too many auxiliary variables can lead to convergence issues. One solution that provided the same power and results was to use an average of complete items and only include individual incomplete items as auxiliary variables (Mazza et al., 2015). In terms of models with parcels, this finding suggests that when parcels are included in a model using FIML to handle missing data, one advisable approach is to include individual items that have missing values as auxiliary variables. This approach allows for the other sources of variance that have been isolated within the parcels to inform MAR relationships that may exist. If using this method, proration, where nonmissing items are averaged although some are missing, should be avoided. Proration assumes that missing items and nonmissing items have similar distributional properties and are equivalent to a within-person mean imputation, where each participant's missing item scores within a given scale would be substituted with the mean of their nonmissing scores on that scale. The assumptions underlying this practice are often not tenable and, just like for mean imputation at the sample level, proration is associated with bias even under MCAR data (Lee et al., 2015; Mazza et al., 2015; Schafer & Graham, 2002). Thus, in an analysis with parcels in the main model and individual items as auxiliary variables, participants with any item missing on a given parcel would have a missing score on that parcel.

To avoid proration of parcels, a conditional statement can be used to create a parcel only when all items for that parcel are complete; otherwise, the parcel would not get computed, and the parcel would remain missing. As with scales, using the items with missing data to inform the parcel-level imputation would provide important auxiliary information for the parcel of interest. Here, using the R-based PcAux package to extract component scores from the entire dataset and using them as a core set of auxiliary variables allows circumscribed imputation such that the set of parcels for a given construct can be imputed as a set and the items with missing information can also be included to inform the missing information of the parcel. By the same token, using PcAux also has the advantage that the set of items for a scale can be imputed as a set so that the within-scale correlations among the items is represented along with all the information that was contained in the dataset and which is represented in component scores that PcAux generates. Even here, however, a scale with lots of items may have convergence issues but less likely with a parcel-level imputation. For additional information on PcAux, which implements the approach introduced by Howard et al. (2015), please visit statscamp.org/resources/PcAux.

5 Parceling in the Literature

In order to have a better idea of the prevalence of parceling in the developmental literature as well as the state of reporting in studies using parceling, we reviewed recent articles published in developmental science. Four hundred quantitative empirical articles were randomly selected from all articles published in 2020 in ten developmental journals covering a variety of research fields and impact factors: *Applied Developmental Science, Child Development, Child Psychiatry and Human Development, Development and Psychopathology, Developmental Psychology, Developmental Science, Early Human Development, Infant Behavior and Development, International Journal of Behavioral Development*, and Journal of *Developmental and Behavioral Pediatrics* (see supplementary materials for details on study selection and full list of studies reviewed). For each article, we took note of five methodological questions, going to the next one only when the previous one was fulfilled: (1) did the authors use SEM to analyze their data?; (2) did the authors use latent factors in their SEM analyses?; (3) were there more than three potential indicators in at least one latent factor?; (4) did the authors use parceling? As can be seen in Figure 12, seven of the studies reviewed used parceling, which represents 1.75 percent of all studies reviewed, 6.14 percent of studies using SEM to analyze their data, and 16.28 percent of studies using latent factors with more than three potential indicators. Of note, 54.39 percent of studies using SEM did not use latent factors. There are many instances where using latent factors may be less appropriate for a study, for example on some single indicators (e.g., score on an executive function task, score on an observation scale) or scales with clinical/diagnostic computing guidelines (e.g., PROMIS® scales; Cella et al., 2010; Pilkonis et al., 2011). Studies using multi-item or multi-indicator scales,

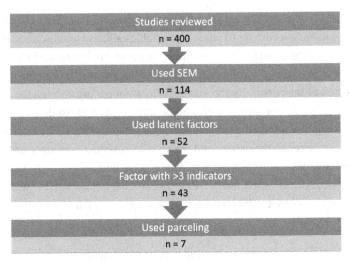

Figure 12 Analytic methods used in the studies reviewed

however, are not taking full advantage of the strengths of SEM by forgoing the estimation of latent constructs, which corrects for measurement error and reduces bias in parameter estimates (Bollen & Noble, 2011). In longitudinal studies and studies examining multiple groups, latent constructs also allow testing the critical assumption of measurement invariance over time or between groups.

Turning first to the seven studies using parceling, the technique was used for estimating a variety of latent constructs frequently examined in developmental science, including parental practices, expectations and bonding (Hopkins et al., 2020; Mathieu et al., 2020; Takacs et al., 2020; Wei et al., 2020), general and specific internalizing and externalizing symptoms (Jambon & Smetana, 2020; Motti-Stefanidi et al., 2020; Rodriguez et al., 2020), child temperament (Takacs et al., 2020), and adolescents' perception of their parents' goals for them (Wei et al., 2020).

Two studies used the factor loadings from an exploratory factor analysis (EFA) to inform a balancing parceling technique (Mathieu et al., 2020; Wei et al., 2020). Two other studies used parceling techniques for multidimensional scales, with one opting for facet-representative parcels (Rodriguez et al., 2020), and the other opting for domain-representative parcels (Jambon & Smetana, 2020). The other studies did not specify the parceling technique used, although one indicated that a difficult temperament scale was parceled into its four subscales (negative affect, dullness, impredictability, and unadaptability; Takacs et al., 2020), from which we can deduct that facet-representative parcels were computed, with the resultant latent construct representing a general difficult temperament factor common to all subscales.

While parceling was likely advantageous in the modeling process of the seven studies, complete reporting of the parceling strategies and decision process was often lacking. Parceling is advantageous when thoughtfully implemented in an analytic plan, and parceling strategies should be fully transparent so that the scientific community can evaluate their appropriateness and facilitate open science and study replication. This transparency should include results of preliminary analyses used to inform parceling strategies (e.g., preliminary item-level EFAs or CFAs), a rationale for the parceling technique and the number of parcels chosen, and details about the items combined in each parcel. When lack of space precludes the inclusion of full details on a parceling strategy, readers can easily be referred to online supplementary materials, which allow the availability of all methodological and analytical details without restrictions on length.

In aiding the implementation of parceling in future developmental studies, we highlight two studies that can be used as examples of parceling and its reporting (Jambon & Smetana, 2020; Mathieu et al., 2020): In computing unidimensional parcels, a CFA was fit to examine the factor structure of the Egna Minner Beträffande Uppfostran (EMBU) child version (Gruner et al., 1999) and parent version (Castro et al., 1997), which are questionnaires measuring perceived parental rearing behaviors that include four scales (i.e., emotional warmth, overprotection, rejection, and anxious rearing; see Mathieu et al., 2020). The results of an EFA were used to inform balanced parceling, which reduced eight to nine item-level indicators per subscale to three parcel-level indicators per scale. They used their latent factors with parcel-level indicators in their analyses to compare factor structures (i.e., a four-factor model, a higher-order model, and a three-factor model where anxious rearing and overprotection were combined into a control factor). As an example with multidimensional parcels (Jambon & Smetana, 2020), the authors estimated latent constructs of physical and relational aggression. Each aggression scale had two subscales: proactive and reactive aggression, and parcels were constructed by averaging one proactive item with one reactive item, yielding domain-representative parcels. The authors provide rationale for their decisions, indicating that reactive and proactive aggression were highly correlated and did not seem to represent different constructs, which led to constructing their parcels with one item of each. This parceling approach reduced the six item-level indicators down to three parcel-level indicators for each construct.

Regarding missing data, most studies did not provide any information regarding how missing data were handled in the parcels, either not providing any information about missing data or detailing missing data rates and handling in the main analyses, but with no information about how it was handled in the construction of the parcels. One study (Hopkins et al., 2020) seems to have used the missing data techniques recommended earlier, in that multiple imputation was used before all analyses, and seems to have been done at the item level (i.e., before parceling), although this was not explicitly stated. As noted in many reviews on missing data reporting and treatments (e.g., Bodner, 2006; Lang & Little, 2018; Peugh & Enders, 2004; Rioux & Little, 2021; Schlomer et al., 2010), poor missing data reporting is an ubiquitous problem in all studies (thus not unique to studies using parceling) and details on missing data rates and missing data handling should be provided in the main manuscript or in supplementary materials. Extra care should be taken in studies using parceling, where details on missing data handling should be given both for item-level missing data used to create parcels and for the main analyses.

Beyond the seven studies that explicitly used parceling, some studies that did not use parceling used an analytical scheme that could be considered an analog to parceling. Indeed, studies sometimes aggregate subscales to use as latent factor indicators, which is analogous to using a facet-representative parceling technique (e.g., Rodriguez et al., 2020; Takacs et al., 2020). For example, one study aggregated questionnaire subscales for use as indicators for latent constructs of familism, parent–child relationship, and support-seeking coping (Stein et al., 2020), and another used aggregated scores on four stress domains (life stress, contextual stress, personal stress, and interpersonal stress) as indicators for a maternal prenatal stress construct (Cortes Hidalgo et al., 2020). Using subscale scores as indicators can intuitively make sense. As explained for facet-representative parceling, this approach is appropriate if the aim is to capture only the common variance between subscales. If the authors aim to capture both the common and facet variances, however, a domain-representative parceling technique could have been favored over using subscale scores as indicators. It is thus important to clearly formulate what the latent construct should represent and to make sure any data aggregation at the indicator-level fit the operationalization of the construct.

Our review also found that some studies highlighted limitations in their analyses that could have been addressed by using parcels. For example, one study indicated that they eliminated items with factor loadings under .40 from their measurement model to help lower the number of parameters in the model (Herman et al., 2020). Parceling would also reduce the number of parameters and would also conserve the construct variance in the indicators with lower factor loadings while reducing their unique variance. Two studies cited small sample sizes as reasons for not testing invariance (Syed et al., 2020, n = 138; Yu & Kushnir, 2020, n = 48). As detailed in Section 2.3.4, parceling can be advantageous when using SEM in small samples because it reduces parameter estimates and increases indicators' reliability.

Overall, our review shows that although globally parceling is used in a small fraction of developmental studies, it is used in a nonnegligeable portion of studies using latent factors in a SEM framework. More studies could certainly benefit from the numerous advantages of parceling; however, it is important to implement parceling in a thoughtful and transparent manner, by choosing a parceling method well suited to the analyses on hand and fully reporting the parceling method employed. Some of the studies reviewed can help the reader with examples using parcels in developmental research.

6 Conclusion

As we have discussed, using item parcels in any domain of research has numerous advantages when done thoughtfully and with clear understanding of the item uniquenesses. These advantages are particularly true in the context of developmental research where longitudinal models are commonly fit to data. Because the size of longitudinal models grows rapidly as more time points are entered, the challenges of estimating them at the item-level are dramatically reduced when item parcels are used instead. Although there is some literature that is critical of item parcels (e.g., Crede & Harms, 2019; Marsh et al., 2013; Rigdon et al., 2019), we have provided a comprehensive overview of why a researcher would benefit from the use of parceling, including the merits of their use, and the conditions in which parcels are particularly useful for developmental scientists. In the end, the careful, thoughtful, and transparent use of parcels is easily justified and well supported in the quantitative literature (e.g., Little et al., 2013; Rhemtulla, 2016; Sass & Smith, 2006). By aiding in the estimation of large structural equation models, parceling is one of many analytic tools that can contribute to our understanding of complex developmental processes.

References

Achenbach, T. M. (1991). *Manual for the youth self-report form and 1991 profile*. Burlington, VT: Department of Psychaiatry, University of Vermont.

Anderson, J. C., & Gerbing, D. W. (1984). The effect of sampling error on convergence, improper solutions, and goodness-of-fit indices for maximum likelihood confirmatory factor analysis. *Psychometrika, 49*(2), 155–173. http://doi.org/10.1007/bf02294170

Bagozzi, R. P., & Edwards, J. R. (1998). A general approach for representing constructs in organizational research. *Organizational Research Methods, 1* (1), 45–87. http://doi.org/10.1177/109442819800100104

Bandalos, D. L. (2002). The effects of item parceling on goodness-of-fit and parameter estimate bias in structural equation modeling. *Structural Equation Modeling, 9*(1), 78–102. http://doi.org/10.1207/s15328007sem0901_5

Bandalos, D. L., & Finney, S. J. (2001). Item parceling issues in structural equation modeling. In G. A. Marcoulides & R. E. Schumacker (Eds.), *New developments and techniques in structural equation modeling* (pp. 269–296). Mahwah, NJ: Lawrence Erlbaum Associates.

Barrett, P. T., & Kline, P. (1981). The observation to variable ratio in factor analysis. *Personality Study and Group Behavior, 1*(1), 23–33.

Bentler, P. M. (1990). Comparative fit indexes in structural models. *Psychological Bulletin, 107*(2), 238.

Bodin, D., Pardini, D. A., Burns, T. G., & Stevens, A. B. (2009). Higher order factor structure of the WISC-IV in a clinical neuropsychological sample. *Child Neuropsychology, 15*(5), 417–424. http://doi.org/10.1080/0929704080 2603661

Bodner, T. E. (2006). Missing data: Prevalence and reporting practices. *Psychological Reports, 99*(3), 675–680. http://doi.org/10.2466/pr0.99.3.675-680

Bollen, K. A. (1989). *Structural equations with latent variables* (Vol. 210). John Wiley & Sons.

Bollen, K. A., & Noble, M. D. (2011). Structural equation models and the quantification of behavior. *Proceedings of the National Academy of Sciences of the United States of America, 108*, 15639–15646. http://doi.org/10.1073/pnas.1010661108

Boyle, G. J. (1991). Does item homogeneity indicate internal consistency or item redundancy in psychometric scales? *Personality and Individual Differences, 12*(3), 291–294. http://doi.org/10.1016/0191-8869(91)90115-r

Browne, M. W., & Cudeck, R. (1993). Alternative ways of assessing model fit. In K. A. Bollen & J. S. Long (Eds.), *Testing structural equation modeling* (pp. 136–162). Thousand Oaks, CA: Sage.

Byrne, B. M. (2005). Factor analytic models viewing the structure of an assessment instrument from three perspectives. *Journal of Personality Assessment*, *85*(1), 17–32. http://doi.org/10.1207/s15327752jpa8501_02

Campbell, D. T., & Fiske, D. W. (1959). Convergent and discriminant validation by the multitrait-multimethod matrix. *Psychological bulletin*, 56(2), 81.

Carifio, J., & Perla, R. (2008). Resolving the 50-year debate around using and misusing Likert scales. *Medical Education*, *42*(12), 1150–1152. http://doi.org/10.1111/j.1365-2923.2008.03172.x

Castellanos-Ryan, N., & Conrod, P. (2011). Personality correlates of the common and unique variance across conduct disorder and substance misuse symptoms in adolescence. *Journal of Abnormal Child Psychology*, *39*(4), 563–576. http://doi.org/10.1007/s10802-010-9481-3

Castro, J., dePablo, J., Gomez, J., Arrindell, W. A., & Toro, J. (1997). Assessing rearing behaviour from the perspective of the parents: A new form of the EMBU. *Social Psychiatry and Psychiatric Epidemiology*, *32*(4), 230–235. http://doi.org/10.1007/bf00788243

Cella, D., Yount, S., Rothrock, N. et al. (2010). The Patient-Reported Outcomes Measurement Information System (PROMIS) developed and tested its first wave of adult self-reported health outcome item banks: 2005–2008. *Journal of Clinical Epidemiology*, *63*(11), 1179–1194. http://doi.org/10.1016/j.jclinepi.2010.04.011

Cheung, G. W., & Rensvold, R. B. (2001). The effects of model parsimony and sampling error on the fit of structural equation models. *Organizational Research Methods*, *4*(3), 236–264. http://doi.org/10.1177/109442810143004

Coffman, D. L., & MacCallum, R. C. (2005). Using parcels to convert path analysis models into latent variable models. *Multivariate Behavioral Research*, *40*, 235–259. http://doi.org/10.1207/s15327906mbr4002_4

Collins, L. M., Schafer, J. L., & Kam, C. M. (2001). A comparison of inclusive and restrictive strategies in modern missing data procedures. *Psychological Methods*, *6*(4), 330–351. http://doi.org/10.1037//1082-989x.6.4.330

Comrey, A. L. (1961). Factored homogeneous item dimensions in personality research. *Educational and Psychological Measurement*, *21*(2), 417–431.

Cortes Hidalgo, A. P., Neumann, A., Bakermans-Kranenburg, M. J. et al. (2020). Prenatal maternal stress and child IQ. *Child Development*, *91*(2), 347–365. http://doi.org/10.1111/cdev.13177

Costa, P. T., Jr., & McCrae, R. R. (2008). The Revised NEO Personality Inventory (NEO-PI-R). In G. J. Boyle, G. Matthews, & D. H. Saklofske (Eds.), *The SAGE handbook of personality theory and assessment, Vol. 2. Personality measurement and testing* (pp. 179–198). Sage Publications, Inc. https://doi.org/10.4135/9781849200479.n9

Crede, M., & Harms, P. (2019). Questionable research practices when using confirmatory factor analysis. *Journal of Managerial Psychology, 34*(1), 18–30. http://doi.org/10.1108/JMP-06-2018-0272

DeYoung, C. G. (2006). Higher-order factors of the Big Five in a multi-informant sample. *Journal of Personality and Social Psychology, 91* (6), 1138–1151. http://doi.org/10.1037/0022-3514.91.6.1138

Diamantopoulos, A., Sarstedt, M., Fuchs, C., Wilczynski, P., & Kaiser, S. (2012). Guidelines for choosing between multi-item and single-item scales for construct measurement: A predictive validity perspective. *Journal of the Academy of Marketing Science, 40*(3), 434–449. http://doi.org/10.1007/s11747-011-0300-3

Eekhout, I., de Vet, H. C. W., de Boer, M. R., Twisk, J. W. R., & Heymans, M. W. (2018). Passive imputation and parcel summaries are both valid to handle missing items in studies with many multi-item scales. *Statistical Methods in Medical Research, 27*(4), 1128–1140. http://doi.org/10.1177/0962280216654511

Enders, C. K. (2001). A primer on maximum likelihood algorithms available for use with missing data. *Structural Equation Modeling: A Multidisciplinary Journal, 8*(1), 128–141. http://doi.org/10.1207/S15328007SEM0801_7

Enders, C. K. (2008). A note on the use of missing auxiliary variables in full information maximum likelihood-based structural equation models. *Structural Equation Modeling: A Multidisciplinary Journal, 15*(3), 434–448. http://doi.org/10.1080/10705510802154307

Enders, C. K. (2010). *Applied missing data analysis.* New York: Guilford Press.

Enders, C. K. (2017). Multiple imputation as a flexible tool for missing data handling in clinical research. *Behaviour Research and Therapy, 98*, 4–18. http://doi.org/10.1016/j.brat.2016.11.008

Field, A. (2016). *An adventure in statistics: The reality enigma.* Thousand Oaks, CA: Sage.

Galambos, J., & Kotz, S. (1978). *Characterizations of probability distributions: A unified approach with an emphasis on exponential and related models.* New York: Springer.

Gorsuch, R. L. (1988). Exploratory factor analysis. In J. R. Nesselroade & R. B. Cattell (Eds.), *Handbook of multivariate experimental psychology* (pp. 231–258). Boston, MA: Springer.

Gottschall, A. C., West, S. G., & Enders, C. K. (2012). A comparison of item-level and scale-level multiple imputation for questionnaire batteries. *Multivariate Behavioral Research*, *47*(1), 1–25. http://doi.org/10.1080/00273171.2012.640589

Graham, J. W. (2003). Adding missing-data-relevant variables to FIML-based structural equation models. *Structural Equation Modeling*, *10*(1), 80–100. http://doi.org/10.1207/s15328007sem1001_4

Graham, J. W., Tatterson, J. W., & Widaman, K. F. (2000). Creating parcels for multi-dimensional constructs in structural equation modeling. In *annual meeting of the Society of Multivariate Experimental Psychology, Saratoga Springs, NY.*

Gruner, K., Muris, P., & Merckelbach, H. (1999). The relationship between anxious rearing behaviours and anxiety disorders symptomatology in normal children. *Journal of Behavior Therapy and Experimental Psychiatry*, *30*(1), 27–35. http://doi.org/10.1016/s0005-7916(99)00004-x

Hall, R. J., Snell, A. F., & Foust, M. S. (1999). Item parceling strategies in SEM: Investigating the subtle effects of unmodeled secondary constructs. *Organizational Research Methods*, *2*, 233–256. http://doi.org/10.1177/109442819923002

Hau, K. T., & Marsh, H. W. (2004). The use of item parcels in structural equation modelling: Non-normal data and small sample sizes. *British Journal of Mathematical & Statistical Psychology*, *57*, 327–351. http://doi.org/10.1111/j.2044-8317.2004.tb00142.x

Herman, K. C., Hodgson, C. G., Eddy, C. L. et al. (2020). Does child likeability mediate the link between academic competence and depressive symptoms in early elementary school? *Child Development*, *91*(2), e331–e344. http://doi.org/10.1111/cdev.13214

Holzinger, K. J., & Swineford, F. (1939). A study in factor analysis: The stability of a bi-factor solution. *Supplementary Educational Monographs*

Hopkins, J., Gouze, K. R., Lavigne, J. V., & Bryant, F. B. (2020). Multidomain risk factors in early childhood and depression symptoms in 6-year-olds: A longitudinal pathway model. *Development and Psychopathology*, *32*(1), 57–71. http://doi.org/10.1017/S0954579418001426

Howard, W. J., Rhemtulla, M., & Little, T. D. (2015). Using principal components as auxiliary variables in missing data estimation. *Multivariate Behavioral Research*, *50*(3), 285–299. http://doi.org/10.1080/00273171.2014.999267

Hoyle, R. H. (2012). *Handbook of structural equation modeling*. New York: Guilford Press.

Iliceto, P., & Fino, E. (2017). The Italian version of the Wong-Law Emotional Intelligence Scale (WLEIS-I): A second-order factor analysis. *Personality*

and Individual Differences, *116*, 274–280. http://doi.org/10.1016/j
.paid.2017.05.006

Jambon, M., & Smetana, J. G. (2020). Self-reported moral emotions and physical and relational aggression in early childhood: A social domain approach. *Child Development*, *91*(1), e92–e107. http://doi.org/10.1111/cdev
.13174

Joo, H., Aguinis, H., & Bradley, K. J. (2017). Not all nonnormal distributions are created equal: Improved theoretical and measurement precision. *Journal of Applied Psychology*, *102*(7), 1022–1053. http://doi.org/10.1037/apl0000214

Keith, T. Z., Fine, J. G., Taub, G. E., Reynolds, M. R., & Kranzler, J. H. (2006). Higher order, multisample, confirmatory factor analysis of the Wechsler intelligence scale for children-fourth edition: What does it measure? *School Psychology Review*, *35*(1), 108–127. ://WOS: 000202998000008.

Kishton, J. M., & Widaman, K. F. (1994). Unidimensional versus domain representative parceling of questionnaire items: An empirical example. *Educational and Psychological Measurement*, *54*(3), 757–765.

Landis, R. S., Beal, D. J., & Tesluk, P. E. (2000). A comparison of approaches to forming composite measures in structural equation models. *Organizational Research Methods*, *3*(2), 186–207. http://doi.org/10.1177/109442810032003

Lang, K. M., & Little, T. D. (2018). Principled missing data treatments. *Prevention Science*, *19*(3), 284–294. http://doi.org/10.1007/s11121-016-0644-5

Lee, M. R., Bartholow, B. D., McCarthy, D. M., Pedersen, S. L., & Sher, K. J. (2015). Two alternative approaches to conventional person-mean imputation scoring of the Self-Rating of the Effects of Alcohol Scale (SRE). *Psychology of Addictive Behaviors*, *29*(1), 231–236. http://doi.org/10.1037/adb0000015

Lei, P. W., & Shiverdecker, L. K. (2020). Performance of estimators for confirmatory factor analysis of ordinal variables with missing data. *Structural Equation Modeling: A Multidisciplinary Journal*, *27*(4), 584–601. http://doi.org/10.1080/10705511.2019.1680292

Lei, P. W., & Wu, Q. (2007). Introduction to structural equation modeling: Issues and practical considerations. *Educational Measurement: Issues and Practice*, *26*(3), 33–43. http://doi.org/10.1111/j.1745-3992.2007.00099.x

Li, C. H. (2016). Confirmatory factor analysis with ordinal data: Comparing robust maximum likelihood and diagonally weighted least squares. *Behavior Research Methods*, *48*(3), 936–949. http://doi.org/10.3758/s13428-015-0619-7

Likert, R. (1932). A technique for the measurement of attitudes. *Archives of Psychology*, *22*(140), 1–55.

Little, T. D. (2013). *Longitudinal structural equation modeling*. New York: Guildford Press.

Little, T. D. (in press). *Longitudinal structural equation modeling* (2nd ed.). New York: Guildford Press.

Little, T. D., Cunningham, W. A., Shahar, G., & Widaman, K. F. (2002). To parcel or not to parcel: Exploring the question, weighing the merits. *Structural Equation Modeling*, *9*(2), 151–173. http://doi.org/10.1207/s15328007 sem0902_1

Little, T. D., Lindenberger, U., & Nesselroade, J. R. (1999). On selecting indicators for multivariate measurement and modeling with latent variables: When "good" indicators are bad and "bad" indicators are good. *Psychological Methods*, *4*(2), 192–211. http://doi.org/10.1037/1082-989x.4.2.192

Little, T. D., Oettingen, G., & Baltes, P. B. (1995). *The revised control, agency, and means-ends interview (CAMI): A multi-cultural validity assessment using mean and covariance structures (MACS) analyses.* Berlin: Max Planck Institute.

Little, T. D., & Rhemtulla, M. (2013). Planned missing data designs for developmental researchers. *Child Development Perspectives*, *7*(4), 199–204. http://doi.org/10.1111/cdep.12043

Little, T. D., Rhemtulla, M., Gibson, K., & Schoemann, A. M. (2013). Why the items versus parcels controversy needn't be one. *Psychological Methods*, *18* (3), 285–300. http://doi.org/10.1037/a0033266

MacCallum, R. C., & Austin, J. T. (2000). Applications of structural equation modeling in psychological research. *Annual Review of Psychology, 51*, 201–226. http://doi.org/10.1146/annurev.psych.51.1.201

Madley-Dowd, P., Hughes, R., Tilling, K., & Heron, J. (2019). The proportion of missing data should not be used to guide decisions on multiple imputation. *Journal of Clinical Epidemiology, 110*, 63–73. http://doi.org/10.1016/j .jclinepi.2019.02.016

Marsh, H. W., Ludtke, O., Nagengast, B., Morin, A. J. S., & Von Davier, M. (2013). Why item parcels are (almost) never appropriate: Two wrongs do not make a right – camouflaging misspecification with item parcels in CFA models. *Psychological Methods, 18*(3), 257–284. http://doi.org/10 .1037/a0032773

Massé, R., Poulin, C., Dassa, C. et al. (1998). The structure of mental health: Higher-order confirmatory factor analyses of psychological distress and well-being measures. *Social Indicators Research, 45*(1–3), 475–504. http:// doi.org/10.1023/a:1006992032387

Mathieu, S. L., Conlon, E. G., Waters, A. M., & Farrell, L. J. (2020). Perceived parental rearing in paediatric obsessive-compulsive disorder: Examining the factor structure of the EMBU child and parent versions and associations with OCD symptoms. *Child Psychiatry & Human Development, 51*(6), 956–968. http://doi.org/10.1007/s10578-020-00979-6

Matsunaga, M. (2008). Item parceling in structural equation modeling: A primer. *Communication Methods and Measures*, *2*(4), 260–293. http://doi .org/10.1080/19312450802458935

Matsunaga, M. (2010). How to factor-analyze your data right: Do's, don'ts, and how-to's. *International Journal of Psychological Research*, *3*(1), 97–110. http://doi.org/10.21500/20112084.854

Mazza, G. L., Enders, C. K., & Ruehlman, L. S. (2015). Addressing item-level missing data: A comparison of proration and full information maximum likelihood estimation. *Multivariate Behavioral Research*, *50*(5), 504–519. http://doi.org/10.1080/00273171.2015.1068157

McDonald, R. P. (1999). *Test theory: A unified treatment*. Mahwah, NJ: Lawrence Erlbaum Associates.

Montigny, C., Castellanos-Ryan, N., Whelan, R. et al. (2013). A phenotypic structure and neural correlates of compulsive behaviors in adolescents. *Plos One*, *8*(11), 13. http://doi.org/10.1371/journal.pone.0080151

Motti-Stefanidi, F., Pavlopoulos, V., Mastrotheodoros, S., & Asendorpf, J. B. (2020). Longitudinal interplay between peer likeability and youth's adaptation and psychological well-being: A study of immigrant and nonimmigrant adolescents in the school context. *International Journal of Behavioral Development*, *44*(5), 393–403. http://doi.org/10.1177/0165025419894721

Murray, J. S. (2018). Multiple imputation: A review of practical and theoretical findings. *Statistical Science*, *33*(2), 142–159. http://doi.org/10.1214/18-sts644

Nasser, F., & Wisenbaker, J. (2003). A Monte Carlo study investigating the impact of item parceling on measures of fit in confirmatory factor analysis. *Educational and Psychological Measurement*, *63*(5), 729–757. http://doi .org/10.1177/0013164403258228

Nunnally, J. C. (1978). *Psychometric theory* (2nd ed.). New York: McGraw-Hill.

Orçan, F., & Yanyun, Y. (2016). A note on the use of item parceling in structural equation modeling with missing data. *Journal of Measurement and Evaluation in Education and Psychology*, *7*(1), 59–72. http://doi.org/10 .21031/epod.88204

Peugh, J. L., & Enders, C. K. (2004). Missing data in educational research: A review of reporting practices and suggestions for improvement. *Review of Educational Research*, *74*(4), 525–556. http://doi.org/10.3102/00346543074004525

Pilkonis, P. A., Choi, S. W., Reise, S. P. et al. (2011). Item banks for measuring emotional distress from the Patient-Reported Outcomes Measurement

Information System (PROMIS (R)): Depression, anxiety, and anger. *Assessment, 18*(3), 263–283. http://doi.org/10.1177/1073191111411667

R Core Team. (2020). *R: A language and environment for statistical computing.* Vienna: R Foundation for Statistical Computing.

Reddy, S. K. (1992). Effects of ignoring correlated measurement error in structural equation models. *Educational and Psychological Measurement, 52*(3), 549–570. http://doi.org/10.1177/0013164492052003005

Rhemtulla, M. (2016). Population performance of SEM parceling srategies under measurement and structural model misspecification. *Psychological Methods, 21*(3), 348–368. http://doi.org/10.1037/met0000072

Rhemtulla, M., & Hancock, G. R. (2016). Planned missing data designs in educational psychology research. *Educational Psychologist, 51*(3–4), 305–316. http://doi.org/10.1080/00461520.2016.1208094

Rigdon, E. E., Becker, J.-M., & Sarstedt, M. (2019). Parceling cannot reduce factor indeterminacy in factor analysis: A research note. *Psychometrika, 84,* 772–780. http://doi.org/10.1007/s11336-019-09677-2

Rioux, C., Lewin, A., Odejimi, O. A., & Little, T. D. (2020). Reflection on modern methods: Planned missing data designs for epidemiological research. *International Journal of Epidemiology, 49*(5), 1702–1711. http://doi.org/10.1093/ije/dyaa042

Rioux, C., & Little, T. D. (2020). Underused methods in developmental science to inform policy and practice. *Child Development Perspectives, 14*(2), 97–103. http://doi.org/10.1111/cdep.12364

Rioux, C., & Little, T. D. (2021). Missing data treatments in intervention studies: What was, what is, and what should be. *International Journal of Behavioral Development, 45*(1), 51–58. http://doi.org/10.1177/0165025419880609

Rioux, C., Stickley, Z., Odejimi, O. A., & Little, T. D. (2020). Item parcels as indicators: Why, when, and how to use them in small sample research. In R. Van De Schoot & M. Miočević (Eds.), *Small sample size solutions: A guide for applied researchers and practitioners* (pp. 203–214). London: Routledge.

Rodriguez, J. H., Gregus, S. J., Craig, J. T., Pastrana, F. A., & Cavell, T. A. (2020). Anxiety sensitivity and children's risk for both internalizing problems and peer victimization experiences. *Child Psychiatry & Human Development, 51*(2), 174–186. http://doi.org/10.1007/s10578-019-00919-z

Rosseel, Y. (2012). lavaan: An R package for structural equation modeling. *Journal of Statistical Software, 48*(2), 1–36. http://doi.org/10.18637/jss.v048.i02

RStudio Team. (2020). *RStudio: Integrated development environment for R.* Boston, MA: RStudio.

Rubin, D. B. (1976). Inference and missing data. *Biometrika*, *63*(3), 581–590. http://doi.org/10.1093/biomet/63.3.581

Rubin, D. B. (1987). *Multiple imputation for nonresponse in surveys.* New York: Wiley.

Rushton, J. P., Brainerd, C. J., & Pressley, M. (1983). Behavioral development and construct validity: The principle of aggregation. *Psychological Bulletin*, *94*(1), 18–38. http://doi.org/10.1037/0033-2909.94.1.18

Sass, D. A., & Smith, P. L. (2006). The effects of parceling unidimensional scales on structural parameter estimates in structural equation modeling. *Structural Equation Modeling: A Multidisciplinary Journal*, *13*(4), 566–586. http://doi.org/10.1207/s15328007sem1304_4

Schafer, J. L., & Graham, J. W. (2002). Missing data: Our view of the state of the art. *Psychological Methods*, *7*(2), 147–177. http://doi.org/10.1037/1082-989x.7.2.147

Schlomer, G. L., Bauman, S., & Card, N. A. (2010). Best practices for missing data management in counseling psychology. *Journal of Counseling Psychology*, *57*(1), 1–10. http://doi.org/10.1037/a0018082

Seaman, S., Galati, J., Jackson, D., & Carlin, J. (2013). What is meant by "missing at random"? *Statistical Science*, *28*(2), 257–268. http://doi.org/10.1214/13-sts415

Stein, G. L., Mejia, Y., Gonzalez, L. M., Kiang, L., & Supple, A. J. (2020). Familism in action in an emerging immigrant community: An examination of indirect effects in early adolescence. *Developmental Psychology*, *56*(8), 1475–1483. http://doi.org/10.1037/dev0000791

Sterba, S. K. (2019). Problems with rationales for parceling that fail to consider parcel-allocation variability. *Multivariate Behavioral Research*, *54*(2), 264–287. http://doi.org/10.1080/00273171.2018.1522497

Sterba, S. K., & MacCallum, R. C. (2010). Variability in parameter estimates and model fit across repeated allocations of items to parcels. *Multivariate Behavioral Research*, *45*(2), 322–358. http://doi.org/10.1080/00273171003680302

Sterba, S. K., & Rights, J. D. (2017). Effects of parceling on model selection: Parcel-allocation variability in model ranking. *Psychological Methods*, *22*(1), 47–68. http://doi.org/10.1037/met0000067

Syed, M., Eriksson, P. L., Frisén, A., Hwang, C. P., & Lamb, M. E. (2020). Personality development from age 2 to 33: Stability and change in ego resiliency and ego control and associations with adult adaptation. *Developmental Psychology*, *56*(4), 815–832. http://doi.org/10.1037/dev0000895

Takacs, L., Smolik, F., Kazmierczak, M., & Putnam, S. P. (2020). Early infant temperament shapes the nature of mother-infant bonding in the first postpartum year. *Infant Behavior & Development*, 58. http://doi.org/10.1016/j.infbeh.2020.101428

Tarka, P. (2018). An over view of structural equation modeling: Its beginnings, historical development, usefulness and controversies in the social sciences. *Quality & Quantity*, 52(1), 313–354. http://doi.org/10.1007/s11135-017-0469-8

Thompson, B., & Melancon, J. (1996). *Using item "testlets/parcels" in confirmatory factor analysis: An example using the PPDP-78*. Paper presented at the annual meeting of the Mid-South Educational Research Association, Tuscaloosa, AL. https://eric.ed.gov/?id=ED404349

Tomarken, A. J., & Waller, N. G. (2005). Structural equation modeling: Strengths, limitations, and misconceptions. *Annual Review of Clinical Psychology*, 1, 31–65. http://doi.org/10.1146/annurev.clinpsy.1.102803.144239

Tucker, L. R., & Lewis, C. (1973). A reliability coefficient for maximum likelihood factor analysis. *Psychometrika*, 38(1), 1–10. http://doi.org/10.1007/bf02291170

Van Buuren, S. (2018). *Flexible imputation of missing data* (2nd ed.). Boca Raton, FL: CRC Press.

Van De Schoot, R., Schmidt, P., De Beuckelaer, A., Lek, K., & Zondervan-Zwijnenburg, M. (2015). Editorial: Measurement invariance. *Frontiers in Psychology*, 6(1064). http://doi.org/10.3389/fpsyg.2015.01064

Velicer, W. F., & Fava, J. L. (1998). Effects of variable and subject sampling on factor pattern recovery. *Psychological Methods*, 3(2), 231–251. http://doi.org/10.1037//1082-989x.3.2.231

Violato, C., & Hecker, K. G. (2007). How to use structural equation modeling in medical education research: A brief guide. *Teaching and Learning in Medicine*, 19(4), 362–371. http://doi.org/10.1080/10401330701542685

Wei, J., Sze, I. N.-L., Ng, F. F.-Y., & Pomerantz, E. M. (2020). Parents' responses to their children's performance: A process examination in the United States and China. *Developmental Psychology*, 56(12), 2331–2344. http://doi.org/10.1037/dev0001125

Weijters, B., & Baumgartner, H. (2022). On the use of balanced item parceling to counter acquiescence bias in structural equation models. *Organizational Research Methods*, 25(1), 170–180

Widaman, K. F., Ferrer, E., & Conger, R. D. (2010). Factorial invariance within longitudinal structural equation models: Measuring the same construct across time. *Child Development Perspectives*, *4*(1), 10–18. http://doi.org/10.1111/j .1750-8606.2009.00110.x

Widaman, K. F., & Thompson, J. S. (2003). On specifying the null model for incremental fit indices in structural equation modeling. *Psychological Methods*, *8*(1), 16–37. http://doi.org/10.1037/1082-989x.8.1.16

Williams, L. J., & O'Boyle, E. H. (2008). Measurement models for linking latent variables and indicators: A review of human resource management research using parcels. *Human Resource Management Review*, *18*(4), 233–242. http://doi.org/10.1016/j.hrmr.2008.07.002

Yang, C. M., Nay, S., & Hoyle, R. H. (2010). Three approaches to using lengthy ordinal scales in structural equation models parceling, latent scoring, and shortening scales. *Applied Psychological Measurement*, *34*(2), 122–142. http://doi.org/10.1177/0146621609338592

Yoo, J. E. (2009). The effect of auxiliary variables and multiple imputation on parameter estimation in confirmatory factor analysis. *Educational and Psychological Measurement*, *69*(6), 929–947. http://doi.org/10.1177/001 3164409332225

Yu, Y., & Kushnir, T. (2020). The ontogeny of cumulative culture: Individual toddlers vary in faithful imitation and goal emulation. *Developmental Science*, *23*(1). http://doi.org/10.1111/desc.12862

Yuan, K.-H., Bentler, P. M., & Kano, Y. (1997). On averaging variables in a confirmatory factor analysis model. *Behaviormetrika*, *24*(1), 71–83. http:// doi.org/10.2333/bhmk.24.71

Acknowledgements

Parts of this work were supported by the Canadian Institutes of Health Research and the Fonds de Recherche du Québec-Santé through fellowships to Charlie Rioux.

Cambridge Elements ≡

Research Methods for Developmental Science

Brett Laursen

Florida Atlantic University

Brett Laursen is a Professor of Psychology at Florida Atlantic University. He is Editor-in-Chief of the *International Journal of Behavioral Development*, where he previously served as the founding Editor of the Methods and Measures section. Professor Laursen received his Ph.D. in Child Psychology from the Institute of Child Development at the University of Minnesota and an Honorary Doctorate from Örebro University, Sweden. He is a Docent Professor of Educational Psychology at the University of Helsinki, and a Fellow of the American Psychological Association (Division 7, Developmental), the Association for Psychological Science, and the International Society for the Study of Behavioural Development. Professor Laursen is the co-editor of the *Handbook of Developmental Research Methods* and the *Handbook of Peer Interactions, Relationships, and Groups*.

About the Series

Each offering in this series will focus on methodological innovations and contemporary strategies to assess adjustment and measure change, empowering scholars of developmental science who seek to optimally match their research questions to pioneering methods and quantitative analyses.

Printed in the United States
by Baker & Taylor Publisher Services